PALEO

COMFORT FOODS

Cookbook

**Super Quick & Easy,
Gluten-Free
Paleo Comfort Food
Recipes**

Printed in the United States of America.
First Printing, 2013

Table of Contents

PALEO - SPICE MIXES

PALEO - MARINADES

PALEO - DIPS AND SAUCES

PALEO - SALAD DRESSINGS

PALEO - SALADS

PALEO - SOUPS

PALEO - BEEF

PALEO - CHICKEN

PALEO - PORK

PALEO - SEAFOOD

PALEO - SIDE DISHES

PALEO - BREAKFAST

PALEO - SNACKS

PALEO - DESSERTS

Let's do it!

Introduction

Before this book can really begin, we have to ask two questions:

1.   What is "paleo"?

2.   What is "comfort food"?

After all, we should have some idea of the general direction things are going to head in, right?

The paleo diet is the latest food craze to sweep the globe. It's not a "diet" per se; if there's one thing that all the fad diets in the last few decades have taught us, it's that "diets" don't work. The idea of temporarily depriving yourself of certain foods until you reach a weight goal has been shown to be counterproductive. Goals are met, but soon after the pent up urge to eat the "forbidden fruit" overcomes us and before we know it we're back where we started. It's a vicious cycle.

Which is good. If you're a diet foods company.

But for us citizens it's a terrible thing. Not only are we getting nothing out of it, but we're running our poor bodies ragged gaining and losing all this weight. The human body just wasn't built to work that way.

Which brings us to the idea behind the paleo diet.

The Way Things Were 'Meant' To Be

We call it a "diet" because what we eat is our "diet". Only in that sense does the term apply. The paleo diet endeavors to get us to eat only those foods which our bodies are "meant" to eat. The things early humans ate when our race was not surrounded by heaps of plastic processed foods and civilization was still in its infancy.

Back then, there were no factory farms. No artificial food dyes, no funky additives that gave food a certain color or texture. There were no "products" there was just... food.

The great thing about this approach to eating is that it's so darn intuitive. You already know the difference between products and food. You can see it with the naked eye 90% of the time. Products come in boxes, bags, cans, what have you. Products have labels, brand names and ingredient lists. Food is just food. You look at it, and you know what it is. You can tell (assuming you're at least moderately educated) what's in it. This is not to say that it's always so cut-and-dry. But on the whole, knowing what's paleo is pretty easy.

The one major distinction that we make with the paleo approach is foods that are pre-agricultural and post-agricultural. The agricultural revolution brought food production to a mass scale, making sustenance cheap and widely available, but it also brought with it a wealth of diseases and disorders related to the simple fact that our guts didn't evolve to eat starchy grains and processed sugars. So anything grain-derived, even if it's all natural, is not paleo. Beans, legumes, and other products that were only cultivated and eaten after the agricultural revolution are not paleo.

Pretty much everything else that's all natural *is*. There are a few gray areas, mostly when it comes to dairy and sweeteners.

The trouble with dairy is that on a low carbohydrate diet, dairy becomes harder for the body to process. The body gets used to digesting food differently, and in the course of things certain enzymes needed to break down certain foods may not be produced.

The trouble with sweeteners is that almost none of them are truly "all-natural", and even the ones that are tend to inhibit the body's ability to process food efficiently. High intake of sugars – even natural ones – makes your blood sugar more irregular, and this makes your body's built-in weight management system goes haywire.

These things are true for some people, and not for others. The trick is to find what your body will tolerate. If you feel healthy after eating it, and you don't have any digestive issues, and you're still able to lose weight (if you're trying to, anyway) then you're probably okay. People who are going paleo for ethical or general health reasons (rather than as a weight-loss plan) will probably tolerate more things. People who want to lose weight might need to hold off on some things. Take a few weeks, find what your body adjusts to.

Once you know what's paleo *for you,* the world is your oyster. While this approach to food might seem limiting at first, you have to remember that food wasn't always the "zap it in the microwave", "grab and go" convenience it is today. We used to have to *make* our food, *hunt* our food, *gather* our food. Food was a ritual, a ceremony, and being more in touch with it – more aware of it – will remind you how lucky we are to be able to feast on the bounty nature provides. This food-consciousness is one of the greatest rewards we get from the paleo diet. Nothing will make you feel as good as knowing that you are the master of all you eat.

But what about comfort food? What do we mean when we say that?

For the purposes of this book, comfort food is anything that gives you a sense of *home,* a feeling of familiarity that makes the food inviting. Part of this is that it's easy to make. There's nothing inviting about a dish that requires a culinary degree to understand. We paleo people like to keep it simple, and that's what comfort food is all about.

Another aspect of comfort food is that it's satisfying. One of the great things about the paleo diet is that it isn't a crime to feel full every once in a while.   So comfort food is always on the menu.

In this book, we're going to be cooking up recipes that will feed the family. Recipes that stick to your ribs and make you want to go back for seconds. In order to do this, we're going to have to go through some basics (the first few chapters are devoted to that) so that you'll have the tools to whip things up easily. By the time you get to the chapter on salads, you should know how to stock and run a paleo kitchen capable of producing anything your heart desires.

A brief note on ingredients:

As we said before, there are a few gray areas in the paleo diet. Some of these recipes call for cheese, a product which many paleo eaters do not tolerate in their diet. We've worked hard to ensure that all these recipes will feel complete and taste great without the cheese, but we've kept it in the recipe just so you know all the possibilities.

The same is true for raw, organic honey. All the recipes that use it will taste great without it, they'll just have a slightly different character. Raw honey is the most natural sweetener there is, but it's still too sugary for some.

We also use a good amount of coconut milk in this book. The coconut is the paleo dieter's best friend; it's versatile flesh and water provide a bounty of products that we can use to substitute for many of the products we eschew.

When buying coconut milk, or any coconut product, read the label. Some producers make these products with paleo dieters in mind. Others make them for other reasons. If you see anything you aren't sure about, put it back.

Things like carageenan, guar gum and any kind of sugar are not your friend. If you know what an ingredient is, and know it's paleo, you're good. For coconut milk specifically, the best stuff actually comes in cans most of the time, and the only ingredients will be coconut milk and water (sometimes not even water). If, for some reason, you can't find good coconut milk, you can always use homemade almond milk. Check out the first chapter for a great recipe.

We use tapioca flour as a wheat substitute in this book. Tapioca flour is made from the ground root of the cassava plant, and its use goes back long enough that it's considered paleo by most people. It's also completely gluten-free, and doesn't have any of the other problems that grain flours do.

However, if you'd be more comfortable, coconut flour may be substituted anywhere you see tapioca flour. Both are widely available in natural food stores, so just decide what works for you.

When it comes to meats, you want everything to be grass-fed or pasture-raised (which is essentially the same thing, health-wise). Meat or eggs from factory farms are usually pumped full of so many chemicals it's hard to tell where the additives end and the animal begins.

Trust us, you will notice the difference in naturally produced meats. They're tastier, often produced locally (which means they're fresher) and they are so much better for you it's not even funny. If you *must* use processed meats, just make sure to buy them as lean as possible and trim any fat that you can. Most chemical additives build up in fat deposits, so you can manage your intake with a little vigilance.

Another ingredient worth mentioning is alcohol. We don't use much in this book, but that doesn't mean you won't want a drink every now and then.

Thankfully wine is paleo, so that's always an option.

Any grain-derived booze, however, is out, so unfortunately whiskey, beer, vodka, all that stuff has to go. If you must have the hard stuff, there are fruit-derived liquors like grappa and pisco. They mix about as well as vodka in your run-of-the-mill cocktails, and they taste pretty good on their own if you're used to taking it straight up.

If you're going paleo to lose weight, however, it's a good idea to avoid alcohol altogether, or drink only in severe moderation. Alcohol has an effect on your body that inhibits weight loss, not to mention it's the usual fuel for bad decisions. So if you can stay away, you're better off. If you can't stay away... you might have some of the things to address!

One final note before we begin.

One rule that is generally agreed upon by many paleo people is the 80/20 rule. The idea is simple:

we don't live in a perfect world. Unless you hunt all your own meat and grow or gather all your own fruits and veggies, chances are you're going to come to a situation sooner or later where you won't have a clear paleo option. No problem. That's what the 80/20 rule is all about. So long as you're eating completely paleo 80% of the time, you're good.

Now that doesn't mean you want to fill that other 20% with pizza and candy bars, but if you're in a situation where the lines are blurred (like at a friend's house where the meat s covered in a starchy gravy, or away from home an unable to cook your own meals) then close enough will be good enough.

Don't go overboard, but don't beat yourself up either. If you're a tyrant about your food, it won't be as fun, and the "comfort" aspect will be lost.

With all this in mind, and with an empty stomach, let's get this show on the road!

PALEO

THE BASICS

The title of this chapter says it all. Here is where we're going to show you a few basic recipes to make *ingredients* rather than whole dishes. These things, once mastered, will become staples in your paleo kitchen, and the building blocks of many more complex dishes.

The paleo ethos is one that rewards DIY cooking with rich flavors, increased flexibility and the pride of knowing that you've beaten the mass-market food producers who are pushing poisonous products on you every day.

If you can buy it in the grocery store, chances are you can make it at home and if you *can't*, chances are you don't want to!

Basic Yellow Mustard

One of the simplest condiments there is, mustard is a crucial ingredient in several other sauce recipes. It works as an emulsifier, as well as adding a salty flavor to anything you use it in. Learning how to make your own will help you keep your diet paleo down to the last detail.

This recipe uses tapioca flour as a thickening agent. Tapioca flour is made from the ground root of the cassava plant, whose cultivation predates the agricultural revolution. It is 100% gluten free and can be found at any natural food store.

Ingredients:

1 1/4 cup ground dry mustard seed
1 cup water
3/4 cup white distilled vinegar
2 tsp tapioca flour
1 tsp sea salt
1/2 tsp turmeric
1/4 tsp garlic powder
1/4 tsp paprika

Directions:

1. In a medium saucepan over medium heat, bring water and vinegar to a boil.

2. Add mustard seed, salt, turmeric, garlic and paprika. Whisk vigorously.

3. Whisk in tapioca flour. Allow to simmer for 5 min, or until mixture has a thick, paste-like texture.

4. Chill at least 2 hours before using. Store in an airtight container. Keeps up to 1 month.

5. Tip: to make whole grain mustard, replace about half of the ground mustard with whole mustard seeds.

Yield: about 2 cups.

Mayonnaise

When you're used to the pre-packaged, lily-white variety with the ridiculously long list of artificial ingredients, making mayonnaise at home might seem like it would be hard. Truth be told, with the right equipment and good quality ingredients, you can do it in under 10 min, and it'll taste so much better than the store bought stuff that you'll never want to go back.

This recipe calls for grapeseed oil, a relatively cheap and light-flavored cold-pressed oil that should be a staple in any paleo kitchen. Olive oil may be used, but it will yield a mayonnaise with a very strong olive oil flavor.

Ingredients:

1 tsp mustard
2 tbsp white wine vinegar
1 tbsp fresh-squeezed lemon juice
1 tsp salt
2 egg yolks
1 1/2 cups grapeseed oil

Directions:

1. In a large mixing bowl combine first five ingredients. Using an electric hand mixer or a whisk (if you're a really good whisker!) whip ingredients together until they reach a frothy consistency.

2. Add oil a few drops at a time, whisking constantly. It helps to have a bowl that will stay in place while you are doing this, or to have a helper add the oil. Take your time at first, only add a few drops every few seconds. Once the mixture starts to lighten, you can start adding the oil faster, maybe 2-3 tbsp at a time. Once it reaches a thick, mayo-like consistency, you can add the remaining oil 1/4 cup at a time. When all oil is added, continue to mix for another 1-2 min, just to ensure everything is incorporated and the texture is perfect.

3. Keep in the refrigerator in an airtight container (a mason jar or an old mayo bottle work great) Keeps up to 1 week.

Yield: about 1 1/2 cups.

Ghee (Clarified Butter)

Some paleo reinterpretations just won't work with cold-pressed oil in place of butter. Especially if you're venturing into the world of paleo baking. Some times the flavor or texture of the dish just needs the special touch that butter provides. But strict paleo eaters generally try to stay away from difficult-to-digest milk sugars found in butter and other dairy products. Ghee is the solution.

When the milk solids are removed from butter, the resulting product is pure animal fat – something us paleo people rely on. Making this stuff at home could not be any easier.

Ingredients:

1-2 lbs butter (depending on how much you want)

Directions:

1. In a medium saucepan over low heat, melt the butter. As soon as it's melted you will see the white milk solids separate from the transparent yellow fat. When the butter

begins to boil, this means the water is cooking off. The bubbles will gradually get smaller, until they reach a foam-like consistency. The milk solids will begin to brown and clump together at this point. Once these clumps start falling to the bottom, remove the pan from the heat.

2. Strain the hot butter through a cheesecloth into a heat-safe container (a glass jar works great). Store in the refrigerator as you would butter. Keeps up to 2 months.

Yield: a little less than 2 cups per pound of butter.

Rendered Animal Fat

For those of you who hate to see a bunch of tasty grease go in the garbage after cooking a particularly fatty piece of meat, stop throwing it out! This animal fat is great for cooking savory dishes, and a great paleo cooking aid.

It takes a little patience and a little know-how, but this process will keep your fridge stocked with easy-to-use paleo ingredients that will kick any dish up a notch.

Ingredients:

Trimmings, skin or sinew from any meat.

*Note: it's not generally a good idea to use more than one kind of meat when rendering animal fat. Some fats will have different chemical properties like smoke point, and will also have different flavors.

Directions:

1. When cooking meats, save any trimmings, unwanted skin and sinew from your meat.

2. Place trimmings, etc. in a large stock pot over low heat and allow to cook, stirring often, until fat has liquefied. This will take different amounts of time depending on the ingredients, and the amounts you use.

3. When fat begins to boil, this means the water is cooking out. Allow to boil for 15 minutes. You may want to cover the pot with a mesh grease guard, to prevent mess, but DO NOT cover the pot with a lid, as this will prevent the water form escaping.

4. After about 15 minutes, all water should be boiled off, and fat should not be bubbling as aggressively. If it's still making a lit of fuss and noise, let it go until it calms down, but don't let the trimmings burn.

5. Strain mixture through a mesh strainer into a heat-proof container like a glass bowl.

6. Strain mixture again through a cheesecloth into your storage container. A mason jar is ideal.

7. Refrigerate up to 1 week.

Yield: variable.

Beef Stock

Beef stock is a great cooking aid; it's good for a lot more than beef stew! Using a small amount of this in place of cooking oils will bring a burst of flavor to any vegetable side without adding much in the way of calories. We paleo eaters may not have to count calories, but every now and then it's still good to lighten things up a bit.

This recipe is naturally very flexible. Feel free to experiment with different aromatics until you arrive at a stock that fits your tastes best.

Ingredients:

Bones, and trimmings from any cut of beef.
*Note: Use the leftover bones and uneaten meat from a beef dish for even more flavor.
1 onion, halved
2 stalks celery, roughly chopped
2 cloves garlic (or more, if desired)
1 bay leaf
2-3 pods whole allspice
1 tsp whole coriander seed

Directions:

1. Add all ingredients to a large stock pot. Cover with water.

2. Allow to boil over medium heat for 1 hour. Stock is done when it is deep brown in color.

3. Strain with a mesh strainer or colander. Store in an airtight container. Keeps up to 1 week in the refrigerator, 3 months when frozen.

   Yield: variable, up to 1 gallon.

Chicken Stock

Chicken stock is another great cooking aid. Starchy root vegetables take it in like an old friend and end up twice as flavorful. It's a great starting point for healthy sauces, and a good substitute for cooking oils when you're craving something a little lighter.

As with the beef stock, the aromatics you use are up to you. This is our favorite combination.

Ingredients:

Bones, skin, trimmings and uneaten meat of 1 whole chicken
1 onion, halved
2 stalks celery, roughly chopped
2 cloves garlic
1 bay leaf
1 sprig fresh thyme
2-3 leaves fresh sage

Directions:

1. Add all ingredients to a large stock pot. Cover with water.

2. Allow to boil over medium heat for 1 hour. Stock is done when it is mellow gold in color.

3. Strain with a mesh strainer or colander. Store in an airtight container. Keeps up to 1 week in the refrigerator, 3 months when frozen.

   Yield: variable, up to 1 gallon.

Almond Milk

Almonds are one of those things that many paleo eaters would do best to eat in moderation, however, tree nuts are definitely an important part of a paleo diet. Additionally, our friend the coconut may provide a number of substitutions for traditional products, but when it comes to dairy there are just some things that you'd rather have without the coconut flavor.

Home made almond milk is so easy you'll wonder why you haven't been making it for years. It's richer and creamier than the store-bought junk, and it yields a usable amount of almond meal as well; which is great if you're into paleo baking.

Ingredients:

    1 cup raw almonds
    2 cups filtered water
    Raw, organic honey (optional)

Directions:

    1. Place your almonds in a resealable container
       and cover them with water. Soak at least

overnight, up to 2 days. The longer you soak them, the creamier the resulting milk.

2. Drain and thoroughly rinse your almonds after they are done soaking. Add them to a blender or food processor.

3. Pour in the 2 cups of water and blend for 1 minute. Almond milk should be a slightly brownish off-white color.

4. Strain your almond milk through a cheesecloth into a resealable airtight container (again, mason jars are great for this). Keeps in the refrigerator up to 3 days.

5. If you're using the leftover almond meal, dry it thoroughly by pressing with the cheesecloth, then spread it on a baking sheet in a thin layer and put it in the oven on the lowest setting. Roast with the oven door slightly open for about 10 min, or until almond meal is dry.

Yield: about 2 cups almond milk and 1 cup almond meal.

PALEO

SPICE MIXES

The problem with store bought spice mixes is that they nearly always contain something you don't want; too much salt, msg, some unidentifiable anti-caking agent... Who needs all that stuff? Those spice mixes are *products,* not food.

Besides, does it really save you that much time and effort to let a factory throw the spices together? And if you really do need to be able to season on the fly, what's stopping you from throwing together a big batch of the seasoning mix you use most and keeping it in the cupboard?

Here are just a few of the most versatile seasoning mixes, all of which you can whip up just by pouring the ingredients into a jar and shaking. It's that easy!

Taco Seasoning

When you're taking things south of the border, you need some good authentic taco seasoning. This little ditty will beat the msg-laden pants off any packaged mix in the spice aisle.

Ingredients:

3 tbsp ground cumin
2 tbsp chili powder
2 tbsp sea salt
2 tsp black pepper
1 tsp onion powder
2 tsp paprika
1 tsp turmeric
1 tsp dried oregano

Directions:

1. Mix all ingredients in a bowl or jar. Use on chicken, fish or ground beef.

Yield: about 1/3 cup.

Cajun Seasoning

If you're craving a nice piece of blackened salmon or some spicy grilled shrimp, nothing is quite as good as a classic Cajun seasoning mix. It brings the fire to any dish!

Ingredients:

1 tbsp salt
1 tbsp garlic powder
1 tbsp paprika
2 tsp black pepper
2 tsp onion powder
1 tsp cayenne
1 1/2 tsp dried oregano
1 1/2 tsp dried thyme
1 tsp crushed red pepper

Directions:

1. Mix all ingredients in a bowl or jar. Use on chicken and all seafood.

   Yield: about 1/3 cup.

Kansas City Style BBQ Rub

Not just good for rubbing on smoked meats, this particular blend of seasonings adds a much needed kick to grilled chicken breasts or even bone-in steaks.

Ingredients:

2 tbsp salt
3 tbsp smoked paprika
2 tbsp ground cumin
2 tbsp chili powder
2 tbsp ground mustard
1 tbsp garlic powder
1 tbsp onion powder
1 tbsp ground coriander
1 tbsp cayenne
1 tbsp black pepper
2 tsp ground sage
2 tsp celery seed
1 tsp ground thyme

Directions:

1. Mix all ingredients in a bowl or jar. Use on chicken, beef, or pork.
Yield: about 3/4 cup.

Italian Seasoning

This one might seem too simple to even warrant a recipe, but we have to admit that when we first started cooking that little bottle of mixed green was an enigma to us, so we might as well lay it all on the table just in case.

Ingredients:

1 tbsp salt
1 tbsp black pepper
1 tbsp dried parsley
1 tbsp dried oregano
1 tbsp dried thyme
1 tsp rubbed sage

Directions:

1. Mix all ingredients in a bowl or jar. Use on chicken, or in home made tomato sauce.

Yield: about 1/4 cup.

PALEO

MARINADES

Nothing brings a plain piece of meat to flavor town quite like a delicious marinade. If you've got the patience and wherewithal to think ahead and marinate your meat, you can enjoy an endless variety of variations on your favorite cuts. If you're so inclined, you might never eat the same piece of meat twice!

The key to marination is time; time for the acid to break down the cells in the meat and carry your flavors deep within. When you cook up your meat, it's become something totally different.

Here we've given you just a glimpse into the world of what's possible.

This handful of foundational recipes should be a jumping-off point, from which you'll travel to a world of unique dishes!

BBQ Marinade

If you don't have a smoker, but crave the robust and flavorful taste of barbecued meat, this marinade is your shortcut to greatness. This recipe calls for honey, which some paleo dieters may not tolerate, but it's plenty good without it!

Ingredients:

2 cloves garlic, minced
1/2 onion, diced
1/2 cup, plus 1 tbsp grapeseed oil
1/4 cup all-natural apple juice
1/4 cup apple cider vinegar
1/4 cup coconut aminos
2 tbsp raw, organic honey
1 tbsp salt
1 tbsp black pepper
1 tbsp smoked paprika
2 tsp roasted ground cumin
2 tsp roasted coriander seed
2 tsp chipotle chili powder
2 tsp ground mustard
1 tsp cayenne
1 tsp ground thyme
1 tsp celery seed

Directions:

1. In a medium saucepan over high heat, sautee the onion and garlic in the 1 tbsp grapeseed oil

2. When onions are nicely charred, add remaining ingredients. Bring to a simmer, whisking frequently.

3. Pour over meat and marinate at least 4 hours, up to 2 days in refrigerator.

Yield: enough for 2 lbs of meat

Asada Marinade

With a blast of cumin and cilantro, this marinade lets you know where it comes from! Great on chicken or beef flap meat, this marinade creates that cantina flavor with a minimum of fuss.

Ingredients:

1/2 onion, diced
2 cloves garlic, minced
1 jalapeno, ribs and seeds removed
1 jalapeno, chopped
1/2 cup plus 2 tbsp olive oil
Juice and zest of 1 lime
Juice and zest of 1 orange
1/4 cup fresh cilantro, packed
3 tbsp ground cumin
1 tsp ground coriander seed
1 tsp salt
1 tsp black pepper

Directions:

1. In a small skillet over high heat, sautee the garlic, onion and jalapeno in the 2 tbsp olive oil.

2. While vegetables are sauteeing, add remaining ingredients to a food processor or blender.

3. When vegetables are well charred, add to food processor.

4. Blend on high about 1 min, until marinade reaches an even consistency.

5. Pour over meat and marinate at least 4 hours, up to 2 days in the refrigerator. If using on seafood, do not marinate more than 2 hours.

Yield: enough for 2 lbs of meat

Basic Greek Marinade

Ask any Greek; they invented everything, including marination! This recipe is sure to add a welcome burst of herbaceous flavor to your next chicken or lamb dish. Also great on game meat.

Ingredients:

1/2 cup olive oil
1/4 cup white wine vinegar
1/4 cup fresh basil, chopped
1/4 cup fresh oregano, packed
1 tbsp fresh thyme, chopped
1 tbsp fresh sage, chopped
3 cloves garlic, minced
1 tsp black pepper
1 tsp salt

Directions:

1. In a small mixing bowl, combine all ingredients and whisk until well combined.

2. Pour over meat and marinate at least 4 hours, up to 2 days in the refrigerator. If using on seafood, do not marinate over 2

hours.

Yield: enough for 2 lbs of meat

Asian Marinade

When you're craving teriyaki, this sweet and savory marinade is the ticket. With natural sweetness from fruit, you can have your Asian dishes the way you like them without all the processed nonsense in takeout.

Ingredients:

1 very ripe peach, peeled and smashed
1/2 cup coconut aminos
2 tbsp sesame oil
1 tbsp rice vinegar
2 cloves garlic, minced
2 tsp salt
1 tsp black pepper
1 tsp fresh ginger, grated
1/8 tsp ground clove
1/8 tsp ground allspice

Directions:

1. Add all ingredients to a food processor or blender and blend about 1 minute, until it reaches a smooth texture.

2. Pour over meat and marinate t least 4 hours,
    up to 2 days in the refrigerator.

Yield: enough for 2 pounds of meat.

Mojito Marinade

This minty, tangy marinade is amazing on chicken, but also goes well with lamb or game meat. Fresh mint is a great herb to have in the kitchen, and adds a unique twist to almost any dish.

This recipe calls for alcohol, which is not tolerated by some paleo eaters. Don't worry, it's just as flavorful without it!

Ingredients:

1/2 cup grapeseed oil
Juice and zest of 2 limes
1/2 cup fresh mint, chopped
1 splash white rum (optional)
1 tsp salt
1 tsp black pepper

Directions:

1. Add all ingredients to a small mixing bowl and whisk until well combined.

2. Pour over meat and marinate at least 4 hours, up to 2 days in the refrigerator. If

using on seafood, do not marinate more than 2 hours.

Yield: enough for 2 pounds of meat

Mustard Marinade

This salty and flavorful marinade is the perfect thing for pork chops or a tougher cut of beef. It will impart an earthy flavor that everybody will love!

This recipe calls for honey, but it can be made without for those who do not tolerate any sweets.

Ingredients:

1/2 cup grapeseed oil
1/4 cup whole grain mustard (refer to the recipe in Chapter 1)
Juice and zest of 1 lemon
2 tbsp raw, organic honey
2 tbsp apple cider vinegar
1 tbsp ground coriander
1 tsp turmeric
1 tsp paprika
1 tsp cayenne
1 tsp salt
1 tsp black pepper

Directions:

1. Add all ingredients to a small mixing bowl

and whisk until well combined.

2. Pour over meat and marinate at least 4 hours, up to 2 days in the refrigerator.

Yield: enough for 2 pounds of meat.

Coconut Lime Marinade

This Asian-inspired marinade is great on robust fish like tuna or swordfish. The creamy flavor of coconut milk and citrusy bite of lime are also wonderful on chicken.

Ingredients:

1/2 cup coconut milk
1/2 cup water
Juice and zest of 2 limes
2 tbsp coconut oil, melted and slightly cooled
1/4 cup fresh cilantro
1 tsp salt
1 tsp black pepper (optional)

Directions:

1. Place all ingredients in a food processor and blend until smooth.

2. Pour over meat and marinate and marinate at least 4 hours, up tto 2 days in the refrigerator. If using on seafood, do not marinate over 2 hours.

   Yield: enough for 2 pounds of meat.

47

Extra Spicy Marinade

If you like it hot, sometimes you just want to go straight for the fire; and that's what this marinade does! Combining all the best fiery spices into a butt-kicking blend that will perk up any meat, this recipe is sure to challenge even the most stalwart fire-breather.

Ingredients:

1/2 cup grapeseed oil
1 jalapeno
1/4 cup red wine vinegar
2 tbsp coconut aminos
1 tbsp chipotle chili pepper
2 tsp cayenne
2 tsp crushed red pepper
2 tsp salt
1 tsp black pepper

Directions:

1. Char the jalapeno by placing it directly over the fire of a gas stove, or by placing in a 500 degree oven for 5-10 min. Jalapeno should be thoroughly blackened.

2. Remove stem of jalapeno and add to food processor along with all other ingredients.

3. Blend until jalapeno is well diced.

4. Pour over meat and marinate at least 4 hours, up to 2 days in the refrigerator.

Yield: enough for 2 pounds of meat.

PALEO

DIPS AND SAUCES

Sometimes even a great marinade isn't enough. You need something to pour over that meat, or a great sauce to dip those grilled veggies in! Not to mention that sometimes we paleo people miss our favorite party dips. Just because you've decided to rise above the carb-filled, artificial chips, doesn't mean you can't still enjoy some of the world's great dips!

This is a collection of some of the most popular dips and sauces you'll find on all kinds of dishes. Some are quick, some take an investment of time, but all of them are sure to satisfy your saucy side.

Balsamic Mayo

This unique little dip is one of those things that goes great on everything. From grilled peppers and onions, to raw zucchini to chicken and steak, this zesty dip will liven up any plate.

Ingredients:

1/2 cup paleo mayonnaise (refer to the recipe in Chapter 1)
2 tbsp balsamic vinegar
2 cloves garlic, minced
1 tsp dry oregano
1 tsp dry thyme
1 tsp black pepper

Directions:

1. Add all ingredients to a small mixing bowl and whisk until well combined. Serve on grilled vegetables, chicken or steaks.

Yield: about 1/2 cup.

Fresh Salsa

There is such a thing as paleo-friendly store-bought salsa, but why would you want that? When you buy it, you don't *get* to make it! Not only is this salsa way tastier than anything you'll find in any store, but it's actually *quicker* than walking into the store and buying a jar.

Ingredients:

1 pound fresh tomatoes
1/4 onion
1-2 jalapenos (depending on how hot you want it – use habaneros if you're a fire-eater!)
1/4 cup cilantro
Juice and zest of 1/2 lime
salt and pepper to taste

Directions:

1. Roughly chop all ingredients, just small enough so they will fit in the food processor or blender. *For extra flavor, char the peppers and onions directly over the fire of a gas stove, or by putting them in a 500 degree oven for 5-10 min.

2. Add all ingredients to a food processor or blender and blend until desired consistency is reached. For chunkier salsa, pulse 5-10 times, for thinner salsa, blend 1 minute.

3. Serve over Pollo Asada or with raw vegetables for dipping.

Yield: about 1 quart.

Salsa Verde

If you can get your hands on green tomatillos (and almost everyone can these days) then you owe it to yourself to try salsa verde some time soon! This tart and spicy sauce goes great on pork, chicken or beef.

Ingredients:

5-6 medium green tomatillos, husked and rinsed
1 jalapeno, sliced
1/3 cup fresh cilantro
1/4 onion, diced
1 tbsp lime juice
salt and pepper, to taste

Directions:

1. Roughly chop all ingredients, just small enough so they will fit in the food processor or blender. *For extra flavor, char the peppers and onions directly over the firs on a gas stove, or by putting them in a 500 degree oven for 5-10 min.

2. Add all ingredients to a food processor and

blend until smooth, about 1 minute.

3. If serving hot, add blended salsa to a medium saucepan and bring to a simmer, whisking constantly.

4. Serve hot or cold over chicken, beef or vegetables.

Yield: about 1 quart.

Guacamole

Freshly made guacamole is one of the most delicious condiments it's possible to eat. Luckily for us, it's also one of the healthiest! Avocados pack a huge load of nutrients and healthy fats, and they have one of the most craveable flavors out there!

Ingredients:

2 ripe avocados
1/2 tomato, diced
1/4 onion, minced
Juice of 1/2 lime
1 tbsp fresh cilantro, finely chopped

Directions:

1. Slice the avocados in half length-wise and twist to separate. Remove pit by striking with the sharp side of a knife and twisting. Scoop meat from avocado into a medium mixing bowl.

2. Add remaining ingredients and stir with a fork, breaking up any chunks of avocado,

until mixture is smooth. Serve on chicken, beef, braised pork, or veggies

Yield: about 2 cups.

Paleo Hummus

Legumes are one of those post-agricultural foods that the human body never quite learned how to deal with. For this reason, us paleo eaters keep them out of our diets. Unfortunately, this meant hummus was off the menu... until now. Thanks to a clever substitution, we can enjoy this earthy dip on carrots and raw zucchini.

Ingredients:

1 cup raw cashews
1/4 cup tahini
3 cloves garlic
Juice of 1 lemon
1 tbsp olive oil, plus more for drizzling
1 tsp salt
1/2 tsp cumin
1/4 cup almond milk

Directions:

1. Place cashews in a resealable container and cover with water. Soak overnight in the refrigerator.

2. Drain cashews and rinse thoroughly.

3. Place cashews, tahini and garlic cloves in a food processor and blend until it reaches a thick, paste-like consistency.

4. Add lemon juice, olive oil, salt and cumin. Blend until well incorporated.

5. Add coconut milk 1 tbsp at a time until desired texture is reached. For thinner hummus, more may be required.

6. Top with a drizzle of olive oil and a sprinkle of paprika if desired.

Yield: about 1½ cups.

Pesto

Basil is one of the most popular herbs to use, and it's no mystery why. It's exploding with flavor, but light enough to let the flavor of whatever it's used on shine through. Combined with a few classic ingredients and you have a sauce that works as well on grilled mahi-mahi as it does over shredded zucchini "pasta" dishes. This recipe omits the traditional Parmesan cheese, to keep things purely paleo. If you tolerate cheese in your diet, however, by all means add it!

Ingredients:

2 cups fresh basil, packed
1/2 cup olive oil
1/4 cup walnuts
2 large cloves garlic
1 tsp salt
1/2 tsp black pepper

Directions:

1. Place all ingredients in a food processor and blend until smooth. Serve over virtually anything.

Yield: about 2 cups.

Argentinian Chimichurri

A cousin to pesto, chimichurri is a robust, herbaceous condiment that elevates any meat or vegetable dish. The herbs used are somewhat flexible, but good, flat-leaf parsley makes all the difference in the world.

Ingredients:

1/2 cup olive oil
2 tbsp freshly-squeezed lemon juice
2 cloves garlic, minced
1/4 onion, minced
1/2 cup parsley, finely chopped
2 tbsp fresh basil, finely chopped
2 tbsp green onion, finely chopped
2 tbsp fresh thyme, finely chopped
2 tbsp fresh oregano, finely chopped
1 tbsp fresh mint, finely chopped
1 tsp crushed red pepper (optional)
salt and pepper to taste

Directions:

1. Combine all ingredients in a small mixing bowl and mix until everything is evenly

distributed. Serve over steaks, chicken, even fish.

Yield: about 1 1/2 cups.

Basic Tomato Basil Marinara

This is marinara sauce in it's most basic form; a great, slow cooked blend of tomatoes and seasonings. It's a much needed addition to zucchini pasta dishes, and if you slather it over some Nut and Herb Fried Chicken (check out the recipe in Chapter 9!) you've got a delicious paleo approximation of Chicken Parmesan!

This recipe calls for a splash of red wine, but if you don't tolerate alcohol, don't worry! It will be all cooked out by the time you eat it.

Ingredients:

4 pounds roma or plum tomatoes, quartered
2 tbsp olive oil
1/2 cup dry red wine
1 onion, diced
4 cloves garlic, minced
1/4 cup fresh basil, chopped
1/4 tbsp fresh parsley, chopped
salt and pepper, to taste

Directions:

1. In a large stock pot over medium-high heat, sautee the garlic and onions in olive oil until soft.

2. Add tomatoes and wine, season with salt and pepper and bring to a simmer.

3. Reduce heat to low, cover, and allow to simmer 30 min, stirring frequently.

4. Stir in remaining ingredients in and transfer to a blender or food processor. Blend until smooth, then return to pan and simmer on low heat, covered for 1 hour, stirring frequently.

Yield: about 2 quarts.

Buffalo Wing Sauce

Wings are always a great, paleo friendly treat for game day or any day. Making your own buffalo sauce keeps them even friendlier!

Ingredients:

16-18 fresh red chili peppers, seeds and stems removed
1 1/2 cups distilled white vinegar
1 tbsp garlic powder
1 tsp sea salt
1/4 cup ghee

Directions:

1. Add the peppers, vinegar, garlic powder and sea salt to a medium saucepan and bring to a simmer over low heat. Simmer for 15 minutes.

2. Remove from heat and pour into a blender or food processor. Blend until smooth.

3. Return to saucepan and simmer an additional 15 min. Add water if sauce

becomes too thick. You want a runny consistency, like traditional hot sauce.

4. When hot sauce is done, set aside and allow to cool for 30 min.

5. In a fresh saucepan, melt ghee.

6. Add hot sauce and whisk until well combined. Serve over hot wings with celery and carrots.

Hollandaise

Hollandaise is one of those things that seems hard to amateurs, but any chef will tell you is actually very easy. Ghee is just a fancy name for clarified butter, and this classical sauce is just an emulsion of clarified butter and egg yolks. If you've made mayo, you already know how to make an emulsion, so this sauce should be a snap! And did we mention it's good on *everything*?

Ingredients:

4 egg yolks
1 cup ghee, melted
2 tbsp lemon juice
1 tsp salt
1/2 tsp cayenne (optional)

Directions:

1. Make a double boiler by placing a medium glass bowl atop a medium saucepan with about 1" of boiling water in it.

2. Add egg yolks, lemon juice, salt and cayenne to double boiler and whisk until

mixture is slightly frothy.

3. Gradually add the melted ghee, whisking constantly. Like with mayonnaise, you want to start slow, but you can add faster as the emulsion becomes stable.

4. When all ghee is added, continue whisking an additional 30 seconds, to ensure everything is well incorporated. Season with cayenne if desired. Serve over poached eggs, braised meats or grilled veggies.

Yield: about 1 cup

PALEO

SALAD DRESSINGS

Salad dressing is one of those things that, once you make it at home, you'll never want to buy from the grocery store again. The simple fact is, it's *easy,* especially if you have a food processor. Within 5 minutes, you can whip up a dressing that's the perfect compliment for any salad; from a simple mixed green side salad to an elaborate dinner salad with grilled chicken.

Here we have a few of the basics and our favorites. Once you try these, you'll see how easy it is to broaden out into uncharted territory and come up with your own house specialties!

Balsamic Vinaigrette

This is probably the most basic dressing there is; a no-frills, dead simple and delicious vinaigrette. It's the perfect compliment for bitter greens or crunchy iceberg, so no matter what salad you're making, this dressing fits the bill.

Ingredients:

1/2 cup balsamic vinegar
1/2 cup olive oil
2 tsp dried oregano
2 tsp dried thyme
1 clove garlic, minced
2 tsp black pepper
1 pinch salt

Directions:

1. Combine all ingredients in a small mixing bowl and whisk until smooth. Serve over spring mix or drizzled over fresh strawberries.

Yield: about 1 cup.

Ranch

Who are we kidding, this is *everybody's* favorite dressing. It's one of those condiments that goes great on everything; from fresh salads to burgers. With a few substitutions and a blast of fresh ingredients, we're whipping it up paleo style.

Ingredients:

1/2 cup Paleo mayo
1/2 cup coconut milk
1 tbsp lemon juice
1 tbsp ghee, melted
2 tbsp fresh parsley, finely chopped
1 tsp black pepper
1/2 tsp dill weed
1/2 tsp onion powder
1/2 tsp garlic powder

Directions:

1. Combine all ingredients in a small mixing bowl and whisk until smooth. Serve on salads or drizzled on roasted veggies.

Yield: about 1 cup.

Mustard Vinaigrette

If you're looking for something tangy to drizzle over your next salad, give this unique recipe a try. With home made mustard pre-made, it's as quick and easy as can be.

Ingredients:

1/2 cup olive oil
1/4 cup whole grain mustard
1 tbsp apple cider vinegar
1 tsp black pepper
1/2 tsp paprika
1/2 tsp cayenne (optional)
2 tbsp raw, organic honey (optional)

Directions:

1. Combine all ingredients in a small mixing bowl and whisk until smooth. Serve over bitter greens or as a condiment on pork chops.

Yield: about 3/4 cup.

Raspberry Vinaigrette

If you're looking for a sweet and tart option to top a salad full of crispy, savory veggies, raspberry vinaigrette is probably your first thought. This easy-to-follow recipe is sure to please everyone.

Ingredients:

1/3 cup grapeseed oil
1/3 cup red wine vinegar
1/2 cup fresh raspberries
1/2 tsp black pepper
1/2 tsp dried thyme
1 pinch salt

Directions:

1. Add all ingredients to a food processor and blend until smooth.

2. Run mixture through a mesh strainer to remove seeds and solids. Press with a rubber spatula for faster results. Serve over a spring green salad with dried strawberries and red onion.

Yield: about 1 cup.

Ginger Almond Dressing

While peanuts are still off the menu (legumes again!) almonds make a great substitution in this Asian-inspired dressing.

Ingredients:

1/4 cup almond butter
1/4 cup grapeseed oil
1/4 tsp sesame oil
1/4 cup coconut aminos
2 tsp grated fresh ginger
1/8 tsp allspice
salt and pepper to taste

Directions:

1. Combine all ingredients in a small mixing bowl and whisk until smooth. Serve over a lettuce salad with shaved carrot and daikon radish.

Yield: about 1 cup.

Primal Green Goddess Dressing

Green goddess is a salad bar classic that nobody should go without. This recipe uses avocado and a healthy helping of fresh herbs to liven up your next salad.

Ingredients:

1/2 ripe avocado
1/2 cup coconut milk
1/2 cup fresh basil
1/4 cup fresh thyme
1/4 cup fresh sage
1/4 cup fresh mint
1/4 cup fresh tarragon
2 green onions, chopped
2 tbsp olive oil (optional)
1 tsp salt
1 tsp black pepper.

Directions:

1. Add all ingredients to a food processor and blend until consistency is smooth. Serve over a hearty salad of mixed vegetables and nuts. It even goes great on burgers!

Yield: about 1½ cups.

PALEO

SALADS

Now that we have all our building blocks and corner stones in place, let's get on to the real comfort food. But... is salad a comfort food?

We submit that it is. Who doesn't enjoy a nice crisp salad on a hot summer's day? Besides, when we say "salad", we really mean that in the broadest possible sense.

In the last chapter we went through some basic dressings. With a simple salad of fresh vegetables, the dressing really *is* the salad, so there's no reason to enumerate the multitude of combinations of fresh veggies (with a few exceptions). Instead, this chapter focuses more on the types of prepared salads you'd likely see in the deli case at your local grocery store; tuna salad, broccoli salad, etc. What we're aiming for in this chapter is to take some of the deli-case classics and bring them into the paleo fold.

We do also have a few recipes for what you might traditionally call a salad, but we're not going to focus on that too much. If you're looking for a great combination of veggies the best advice is to stick with what's fresh and what's local. Chances are it will all go great together.

Easy Chicken Salad

The king of prepared salads is undoubtedly chicken salad. With the sweet and savory combination of flavors, it's a perfect light summer lunch.

This recipe forgoes the traditional boiling of a whole chicken and goes straight for the breast.

Ingredients:

2 boneless, skinless chicken breasts
3 tbsp salt
Water
1/2 cup paleo mayo (or more)
2 stalks celery, diced
2 tbsp slivered almonds
1/2 cup grapes, halved
1 tsp black pepper
1/2 tsp dill weed
1/4 tsp fresh thyme, chopped
1/4 tsp garlic powder
1/4 tsp ground coriander
salt, to taste

Directions:

1. In a medium saucepan over high heat, bring water to a boil. Add salt.

2. Boil chicken until done, about 20-25 min, depending on the thickness of the breasts.

3. Remove breasts from water and pat dry with a paper towel. Dice to desired size.

4. In a medium mixing bowl, combine chicken with all remaining ingredients and stir until everything is evenly distributed. Serve on almond crackers or atop a bed of shredded lettuce.

Yield: about 2 1/2 cups.

Tuna Salad

Perhaps the simplest of the prepared salads, this is not one to be overlooked. The tangy, fishy flavor is one of a kind.

Ingredients:

1 can (5oz) tuna OR 5 oz fresh tuna steak, fully cooked
1/2 cup paleo mayo (or more)
2 tbsp dill pickle, minced
1 stalk celery, diced
1 tbsp onion, minced
1 tsp black pepper
salt, to taste

Directions:

1. Thoroughly drain canned tuna. Place in a medium mixing bowl and break apart with a fork.

2. Add remaining ingredients and mix until everything is evenly distributed. Serve atop bitter greens or with celery for dipping.

Yield: about 1 cup.

Egg Salad

Another simple recipe that shouldn't be overlooked, egg salad is a delightful and delicious cool lunch item that anyone can whip up in a few minutes.

Ingredients:

6 hard boiled eggs, diced
1/2 cup paleo mayo
2 tbsp dill pickle, minced
1 tbsp onion, minced
1 tbsp red bell pepper, minced
1 tsp dill weed
1/2 tsp ground coriander
1/2 tsp celery salt
1/2 tsp black pepper

Directions:

1. Add all ingredients to a medium mixing bowl ans stir until everything is evenly distributed. Yolks will break apart and mix on their own.

2. Serve in iceberg lettuce cups or on red bell peppers.

Yield: about 1 1/2 cups.

Tabouleh

Tabouleh is a traditional Mediterranean side salad/condiment that is often served with lamb or other spiced meats. We make it paleo by substituting crumbled cauliflower for the traditional couscous.

Ingredients:

2 1/2 cups parsley, chopped, some stems included
Juice and zest of 1 lemon
3-4 cloves garlic, minced
1/2 cup cherry tomatoes, quartered
1/4 onion, minced
1 cup cauliflower crowns
1 tbsp olive oil
Salt and pepper, to taste

Directions:

1. In a medium mixing bowl, combine parsley, lemon zest, garlic, tomatoes and onion. Set aside.

2. Boil the cauliflower stems for 2-3 minutes in

salted water and drain thoroughly. You don't want them too soft, about the texture of al dente pasta.

3. Trim as much stem as possible off the cauliflower.   Ideally, you want only the tips. Place cauliflower in a food processor and pulse to fine crumbs.

4. Add cauliflower to vegetable mixture and mix well.

5. Drizzle with olive oil and season with salt and pepper.

6. Stir in lemon juice just before serving.

Yield: about 3 cups.

Broccoli Salad

Broccoli salad? Is that even a thing? Why yes, yes it is. And it's a good thing. It's a great accompaniment to any lunch dish, from lettuce wraps to hot soup.

Ingredients:

2 cups broccoli crowns, finely diced
1/4 cup slivered almonds
2 tbsp onion, minced
4 strips bacon, crumbled
*Note: You want to get uncured, nitrate-free bacon. If your paleo diet still doesn't tolerate this, a finely minced 1/4 cup of pork shoulder that's been fried in animal fat makes a great substitution.
1/2 cup paleo mayo
salt and pepper to taste

Directions:

1. Add all ingredients to a medium mixing bowl and stir until everything is evenly distributed. Serve with cold grilled chicken or alongside a cup of hot soup.

Thai Coleslaw

Traditional American-style coleslaw is too laden with sugar to really work on a paleo meal plan. But with a few twists, this cool and refreshing dish can transform into a spicy Asian side that still goes great with BBQ!

Ingredients:

3 cups cabbage, shredded
3 carrots, shredded
1 jalapeno
1/4 cup fresh cilantro
1/4 cup fresh basil (Thai basil, if you can get it)
1/2 cup coconut milk
1/2 cup Paleo mayo
Juice and zest of one lime
1/2 tsp ground coriander
1/2 tsp ground ginger
Salt and pepper to taste

Directions:

1. Shred and chop the cabbage, carrots, basil and cilantro.

2. Slice the jalapeno paper-thin on a mandoline. If you don't have a mandoline, just slice as thin as you possibly can.

3. Add coconut milk, mayo, lime juice, lime zest and spices to a large mixing bowl and whisk until well combined.

4. Add vegetables and toss in dressing until thoroughly coated.

Yield: about 3 1/2 cups.

Dried Strawberry Spinach Salad

This is one of only two traditional vegetable salads that we'll be going through, and the real reason is because we just had to stick this simple recipe for drying strawberries *somewhere*. Works great with a variety of dressings, but balsamic vinaigrette is it's natural companion.

Ingredients:

2 cups strawberries, halved, tops cut off
Balsamic vinegar, for drizzling
4 cups spinach
1/2 cup walnuts
1/4 red onion, thinly sliced

Directions:

1. Preheat the oven to its lowest setting.

2. Arrange strawberries on a lightly greased baking sheet, making sure the cut side is facing up. This not only aids absorption of the vinegar, but it keeps the strawberries from sticking to the pan.

3. Drizzle lightly with balsamic vinegar.

4. Place in oven with oven door slightly open for 2 hours. Check them periodically to ensure they aren't getting too hot, especially if you have an older gas oven.

5. When strawberries are dry, remove from oven and allow to cool to room temperature.

6. Toss with remaining ingredients and desired salad dressing.

Yield: about 2 servings.

Chopped Salad

Chopped salad can be made of nearly anything; it's the technique that counts. Here we'll go over one of our favorite combinations, and introduce a technique that will save you a boatload of time.

Ingredients:

1/2 head iceberg lettuce, finely shredded
1 fully cooked grilled chicken breast
4 strips uncured bacon, crumbled
2 hard boiled eggs
1/2 cup broccoli crowns
1/2 cup tomato, diced
1/2 cup cucumber

Directions:

1. Place the lettuce, bacon and tomato in a large mixing bowl. Set aside.
2. Add remaining ingredients to a food processor one at a time. Pulse 3-4 times to chop fine. Do not do this with the tomato, or you will get salsa.
3. After each ingredient is chopped, add to the mixing bowl.

4. Toss with desired dressing

Yield: about 2 servings.

PALEO

SOUPS

There's nothing more comforting than a big bowl of soup, especially during the winter. For paleo eaters, soup can be a new frontier; a place to figure out clever substitutions for the artificial junk in your favorite recipes. In this chapter we'll cover a little of everything, from hearty beef stews to chicken soup to veggie-based soups.

One tip for those who haven't made soup before; Don't be afraid to make a big batch. These recipes can and should be doubled and tripled, because anyone who *has* made soup before will tell you – it's always better on the second day.

Everything we'll be going through is great in the fridge for up to 3 days, and can easily be frozen for months. So fill up those crock pots, stock pots and dutch ovens, and let's get cooking!

Texas-Style Chili

In most of the country chili is usually a kind of bean and tomato based soup that's rounded out with ground meat. Not so in Texas. In fact, if you serve a Texan a bowl of something with beans in it and you call it chili, you'll probably get it right back!

Texas chili is all about the meat and the chili powder. Meaty, spicy and above all *simple;* just the way paleo people like it.

Ingredients:

2 pounds beef chuck, or any tougher, fatty cut of beef
3 cups beef stock
2 tbsp rendered animal fat
1 onion, diced
4 cloves garlic, minced
3 tomatoes, diced
1/4 cup chipotle chili powder
2 sprigs fresh thyme
2 tsp smoked paprika
2 tsp roasted ground cumin
1 bay leaf
1 tsp cayenne (optional)
Salt and pepper, to taste

Directions:

1. Preheat the oven to 300 degrees.

2. In a dutch oven over medium-high heat, melt the animal fat. Sautee the onions, garlic and tomatoes about 5-10 min, until the onions have a little char on them and the tomatoes are beginning to break down.

3. While vegetables cook, dice your meat into 1/2" cubes. Season with salt and pepper, then add to pan.

4. Cook beef until browned on all sides, about 6-8 min.

5. Pour in beef broth and add chili powder, paprika, cumin, bay leaf and cayenne (if using). Tie the fresh thyme sprigs with a little string and set in the broth. You may want to tie the string to the handle of the crock pot to make it easier to fish out later.

6. Cover and transfer the dutch oven to the preheated oven. Cook for 2 hours, checking once during cooking to make sure that the broth hasn't over-reduced. If it has, just add a little water until it reaches the right consistency. Serve piping hot.
   Yield: about 5-6 servings.

Chicken Veggie Soup

While noodles and rice are full of carbs and other nasty things that we paleo eaters try to avoid, there's something about hot chicken soup that will just never stop being good. Luckily, we don't have to give it up, we just have to shift the focus. Instead of a bowl of noodles with a few sad little flecks of chicken floating near the bottom, we can cook up a delicious soup with huge, hearty chunks of chicken and large-cut rustic vegetables. And it's still the best thing for a winter cold.

Ingredients:

2 boneless, skinless chicken breasts
3 tbsp grapeseed oil
3 cups chicken stock
2 carrots, roughly chopped
3 stalks celery, roughly chopped
1/2 onion, roughly chopped
2 medium turnips, cubed
1 bay leaf
2 sprigs fresh thyme
Salt and pepper, to taste

Directions:

1. Preheat the oven to 350 degrees.

2. In a medium skillet over medium-high heat, warm 1 tbsp of the oil.

3. Season chicken breasts with salt and pepper. Cook in skillet 2-3 min, until browned on one side. Flip, then transfer pan to oven and bake 15 min, or until chicken reaches an internal temp of 165 degrees.

4. While the chicken is cooking, add the remaining oil to a dutch oven and heat over medium heat. Add the vegetables and cook 3-5 min, until onions are translucent and carrots are beginning to soften.

5. Deglaze the dutch oven with the chicken broth. Allow vegetables and broth to come to a simmer.

6. Remove the chicken from the oven and roughly dice it. Add it to the soup.

7. Add bayleaf. Tie thyme sprigs up with a little string and place in the broth. You may want to tie the string to the handle of the dutch oven to make it easier to fish out later.

8. Cover and transfer the dutch oven to the preheated oven. Reduce heat to 300 and allow to cook 30 min. Serve piping hot.

Yield: about 5-6 servings.

Beef Stew

Who says beef stew needs to be all about potatoes and a broth thickened with wheat flour? Why can't beef stew be about *beef*?

This beef stew is just that. Beefy! We keep some of the traditional textures in there with a few paleo substitutions, and overall you've got a healthier take on this classic comfort food.

Ingredients:

2 pounds beef stew meat
3 cups beef stock
2 tbsp ghee
1 onion, diced
2 cloves garlic
2 stalks celery, roughly chopped
3 carrots, roughly chopped
1 cup butternut squash, cubed
1 bay leaf
2 sprigs fresh thyme
2 tbsp tapioca flour
Salt and pepper, to taste

Directions:

1. Preheat the oven to 300 degrees.

2. In a dutch oven over medium-high heat, melt the ghee.

3. Add vegetables and sautee 5-10 min, until onions are translucent and carrots are beginning to soften.

4. Season beef with salt and pepper and add to the dutch oven. Cook until browned on all sides, about 5-7 min.

5. Deglaze pan with beef stock. Allow stew to come to a simmer.

6. Add the bayleaf. Tie thyme sprigs up with a little string and place in the broth. You may want to tie the string to the handle of the dutch oven to make it easier to fish out later.

7. Cover and transfer to the preheated oven and cook for 1 hour 30 min. remove from oven and stir in tapioca flour, making sure to mix well. Add more water if necessary, but not much; you want it thick.

8. Return to oven for an additional 30 min. Serve piping hot. *Yield: about 5-6 servings.*

Italian Sausage Stew

If you've ever been to one of those Italian places with the unlimited soup and salad, you probably know the inspiration for this little stew. Pork sausage might not be the first meat one thinks of when one thinks of soup, but treated properly it can make an amazing soup that goes great with anything.

Ingredients:

Sausage Ingredients:

2 lbs ground pork
1 tbsp red wine vinegar
1 tbsp salt
2 tsp pepper
2 tsp fresh Italian parsley
2 cloves garlic, minced
1/4 small onion, minced
1 tsp dried basil
1 tsp dried oregano
1/2 tsp dried thyme
2 tsp paprika
2 tsp crushed red pepper
1 tsp whole fennel seed

Soup Ingredients:

1 onion, diced
2 tbsp ghee
2 medium turnips, cubed
2 cloves garlic, minced
2 cups kale, chopped
4 cups chicken stock
2 cups water
1/2 cup coconut milk
1/2 cup almond milk

Directions:

1. In a large mixing bowl, combine all sausage ingredients and mix with hands until everything is just distributed. Try not to over mix.

2. Cover and refrigerate overnight, up to 24 hours.

3. Preheat the oven to 350 degrees.

4. Heat a dutch oven over medium-high heat. Add ghee and onions and sautee until onions are lightly charred, about 5-7 min.

5. Add the sausage and cook through, about 8-10 min.

6. Add all remaining ingredients except the kale. Cover and transfer dutch oven to preheated oven. Cook 1 hour.

7. Add kale just before serving. Serve piping hot.

Yield: about 5-6 servings.

Gazpacho

Here's a classic cool soup that needs little to no
fiddling with to make it a paleo masterpiece.
Gaspacho is a cold tomato-based soup, and on a hot
summer day there's nothing better. Who says soup
is only good on cold days?

Ingredients:

1 pound ripe tomatoes
2 seedless cucumbers
1/4 onion
2 cloves garlic
1 red bell pepper
1/4 cup fresh parsley, chopped
2 tbsp fresh basil, chopped
2 tbsp fresh cilantro, chopped
1 tsp ground cumin
1/2 tsp cayenne (optional)
1 tbsp balsamic vinegar
Juice of 1 lemon
1 tsp lemon zest
2 tbsp olive oil
Salt and pepper to taste

Directions:

1. Bring a pot of hot water to a rolling boil.

2. Blanch all the vegetables, except the cucumbers, for 10-20 seconds, then cut into pieces just small enough to fit in your blender or food processor.

3. Add all ingredients to a blender or food processor. Blend on high until everything is finely diced and well mixed.

4. Run mixture through a mesh strainer set over a large mixing bowl. Press with a spoon or rubber spatula until all puree has been filtered. Discard any seeds, peels and solids left over in the strainer.

5. Chill soup 2 hours, or overnight before serving.

Yield: about 5-6 servings.

Spiced Carrot Soup

Here's something a little off the beaten path; a warm, hearty carrot soup. With the natural sweetness of carrots and the always-welcome zing of fresh ginger, this soup is something a little different to serve at your next dinner party.

Ingredients:

2 tbsp ghee
1 onion, diced
4 cups chicken stock
1 1/2 pounds carrots, peeled and chopped
1 tbsp fresh ginger, grated
1/4 cup almond milk
1/4 cup coconut milk
1/8 tsp ground nutmeg
1/8 tsp ground allspice
1/8 tsp ground cinnamon

Directions:

1. Melt the ghee in a large stock pot over medium heat. Add the onions and sautee until lightly charred.

2. Deglaze with chicken stock. Add the carrots then bring to a boil. Allow to boil 15-20 min, until carrots are soft.

3. Add remaining ingredients and boil another 5-10 min.

4. Remove from heat and pour into a blender or food processor. You may have to work in batches.

5. Blend until smooth. Garnish with a little fresh parsley. Soup may be served hot or cold.

Yield: about 5-6 servings.

Cauliflower Soup

Once again, this might not be the vegetable you think of when you're thinking of soup. Cauliflower is usually reserved for veggie part trays, but as it happens it can be a handy substitution for the usual carb-laden tubers. This soup, while not quite like potato soup, is sure to satisfy those cravings for a soup that's rich and creamy. Try it cold too!

Ingredients:

3 tbsp ghee
2 stalks celery, chopped
1/2 onion, diced
2 cloves garlic
4 cups chicken stock
1 tsp fresh thyme, chopped
1 tsp fresh tarragon, chopped
1 tsp fresh parsley, chopped
1 medium head cauliflower, chopped
1/4 cup coconut milk
Salt and pepper, to taste

Directions:

1. In a large stock pot over medium-high heat,

melt the ghee. Add onion, garlic and celery, sautee about 5 min, until onions are translucent.

2. Deglaze pan with chicken stock. Add all remaining ingredients and bring to a boil. Allow to boil 20 min, until all vegetables are very soft.

3. Transfer soup to a blender or food processor and blend until smooth. You may have to work in batches. Serve soup hot or cold.

PALEO

BEEF

People who follow a paleo diet are lucky. The center, the very cornerstone of everything we eat is the one thing that most other people deprive themselves of: *meat*. And among meats, beef is surely king.

One of the best things about cooking beef for the paleo palate is that you don't need to do a whole lot of substituting to keep things all-natural. At least, where recipes are concerned. The beef itself is an area that some people find challenging, but we view it as rewarding.

When it comes to the beef you buy, you want it all pasture-raised and grass fed. A lot of what makes beef "bad for you" is the diet that the cows themselves are on. Beef that's raised naturally, on the other hand, is nutritious, and even tastes better than the factory farm produced junk. It may be a mite more expensive, but once you've tried a grass fed beef tenderloin, you'll know it's worth it.

In this chapter we'll go over some of the most popular ways to cook and serve beef. Hopefully after reading through these, you'll start to glimpse the endless possibilities for beef on a paleo diet.

Pot Roast with Butternut Squash

Traditional pot roast relies on carrots and potatoes to round out the meal, but this dish adds a pop of flavor and a sultry texture by bringing butternut squash to the party. You'll be amazed at the way the squash soaks in the rich flavors of the beef, and the way you don't miss the flavorless, starchy potatoes at all.

Ingredients:

2 tbsp rendered animal fat
2 lbs beef chuck roast or other beef roast
4 cups beef stock
2 cups butternut squash, cubed
3 carrots, roughly chopped
1 onion, roughly chopped
4 cloves garlic
2 bay leaves
2 sprigs fresh thyme
Salt and pepper, to taste

Directions:

1. Preheat the oven to 350 degrees.

2. In a dutch oven over medium-high heat, melt animal fat. Add onion and garlic, sautee 3-5 min, until onions are slightly charred.

3. Add beef, brown on both sides, 2-3 min per side.

4. Deglaze pan with beef stock. Add remaining ingredients. Cover and transfer dutch oven to the preheated oven. Cook for 2-3 hours, until beef is fall-apart tender and vegetables are very soft. Serve with broth for dipping.

Yield: 4 servings.

Mustard Crusted Steaks

There's nothing wring with a plain old steak, that's for sure. Beef is pretty tasty with nothing but salt and pepper. But that doesn't mean that a little something extra isn't welcome every now and then. This mustard crust packs a tart, acidic flavor that will boost even the most pedestrian cuts of meat to five-star status. Try it on pork chops too!

This recipe calls for cheese, which is a paleo gray area. Some people do not tolerate it in their diet, but most do in moderation. Trust us, this one's worth it.

Ingredients:

2 steaks of your choice
salt and pepper, to taste
grapeseed oil, for the pan
3 tbsp paleo mayo
1/4 cup whole grain mustard
1/4 cup grated Parmesan cheese
2 tsp lemon juice
2 tsp garlic powder
1 tsp paprika
1 tsp pepper
1 tsp ground coriander
1/2 tsp cayenne (optional)

Directions:

1. Preheat oven to broil.

2. In a small mixing bowl, whisk together mayo, mustard, Parmesan, lemon juice, garlic, paprika, pepper, coriander and cayenne (if using) until it forms a thick paste. Set aside.

3. Season your steaks generously with salt and pepper.

4. Lightly coat a large, heavy bottom skillet with oil and heat over medium heat.

5. When pan is hot, lay steaks in. Cook on one side 3-4 min, depending on the desired level of doneness.

6. Flip the steaks and spread the crust topping on the cooked side of the steak.

7. Transfer pan to broiler and cook an additional 5-6 min, or to desired level of doneness. If your pan will not fit into the broiler, transfer steaks directly to the broiler pan.

Yield: 2 servings.

Twice-Cooked Asian Beef

There's something about that beef you get in those fancy Chines restaurants that's just different than anything you cook at home. This recipe seeks to approximate that flavor while keeping things paleo.

To achieve this, the recipe calls for honey; another one of those gray areas. Raw, organic honey is tolerated by most paleo people in moderation, but this recipe is plenty good without it.

Ingredients:

1 lb beef flank steak or flap meat
2 tsp grapeseed oil
2 tsp sesame oil
1/2 tsp fresh ginger, grated
2 cloves garlic, grated
1/2 cup coconut aminos
1/2 cup water
1/4 cup raw, organic honey
1/4 cup chopped green onions
1/4 cup tapioca flour
1/2 cup coconut oil, for frying

Directions:

1. In a medium saucepan, combine 2 tsp grapeseed oil, 1 tsp sesame oil, ginger, garlic, coconut aminos and honey. Simmer 5-6 min, whisking constantly. Set sauce aside.

2. Slice the beef into thin strips. Dip each strip into the tapioca flour, shaking off any excess. Allow the beef to rest 5 min.

3. In a wok or large, heavy bottom skillet, melt the coconut oil.

4. Fry beef in coconut oil 2-3 min, until slightly dark on edges. Remove from oil and drain on paper towels.

5. Pour oil out of wok or skillet. Add beef back and pour sauce in. Stir-fry for 2-3 min.

6. Add green onions and stir fry an additional minute. Serve over riced cauliflower, or just by itself.

Yield: 2 servings.

Beef Tenderloin, The Right Way

The tenderloin just might be the best cut of beef. It's as tender as the name implies, and it's full of rich, beefy flavor. Filet Mignon is cut form this prized strip of meat, but when cooked whole it can take on a character second to none.

Spices and flavorings are flexible. We've presented this recipe as simply as possible, just to give you an idea of the technique before you get creative with crusts (the mustard crust would be great here!) and flavorings.

Ingredients:

1 beef tenderloin, about 6 oz per guest (you may not have much choice, but this stuff keeps well for about 3 days)
2 tbsp olive oil
1 bunch fresh parsley, chopped
4 cloves garlic, minced
Salt and pepper to taste

Directions:

1. Preheat the oven to the highest setting.

2. In a medium mixing bowl, combine oil, parsley, garlic salt and pepper. Stir until well mixed.

3. Rub mixture on every side of the tenderloin, then arrange tenderloin in a large baking dish. Top with any additional seasoning mixture.

4. Place the tenderloin in the oven and turn the oven off. When the oven is completely cool, your beef will be a perfect medium rare throughout, and it will have already rested! Slice and serve with your choice of condiments.

Yield: variable.

Greek Meatballs

Italian meatballs, while delicious, are usually about half breadcrumbs. Who needs all those carbs getting in the way of our delicious protein? The Greeks, on the other hand, keep it simple with a healthy dose of herbs and just enough egg to hold it all together.

Ingredients:

2 lb ground beef
1/2 onion, minced
2 cloves garlic, minced
2 eggs
1 tbsp fresh basil, chopped
1 tbsp fresh parsley, chopped
1 tbsp fresh oregano, chopped
2 tsp fresh mint, chopped
Salt and pepper, to taste
Coconut oil, for frying

Directions:

1. In a small mixing bowl, beat together eggs, herbs, onion, garlic, salt and pepper. Whisk until everything is well distributed.

121

2. Add the beef and work the egg mixture into the beef with your hands. Try not to overwork the meat, just mix until everything is distributed.

3. In a large, heavy bottom skillet over medium heat, melt enough oil that the meatballs will be a quarter to halfway submerged.

4. Roll the meat mixture into balls about the size of a silver dollar.

5. Add meatballs to oil and fry on all sides, turning occasionally. Serve as an appetizer or with grilled vegetables.

Yield: about 4 servings

Ultimate Paleo Burgers

While a burger doesn't require much thought when it comes to the meat (it's just a specific shape, right?). What makes a paleo burger a *burger* and not a Salisbury steak is how you dress it. Submitted here is one suggestion to make you wonder what was so great about those buns in the first place.

Ingredients:

2 lbs ground beef
Salt and pepper to taste
8 strips uncured bacon
4 eggs
2 tbsp ghee
4 slices of cheese (optional)
1 egg yolk
1/4 cup grapeseed oil
1/4 cup olive oil
1 tsp mustard
3 cloves garlic, grated
1 tsp salt
1 tsp black pepper
1 tsp lemon juice
8 large leafs iceberg or butter lettuce

Directions:

1. Make a garlic aioli: Combine the egg yolk, mustard, salt, lemon juice and garlic in a medium mixing bowl and mix with an electric hand mixture until frothy. Slowly add the oil, drop by drop at first. Whisk constantly until mixture is thick and spreadable.

2. Preheat the oven to 400 degrees.

3. Shape your burger patties and season the outside generously with salt and pepper. Try to work the meat as little as possible to get them into shape.

4. Arrange bacon on a sheet pan with raised sides. Bake the bacon in the oven until crispy, about 15-20 min. remove and drain on paper towels.

5. In a medium skillet over medium heat, melt the ghee. Fry the eggs sunny side up or over easy, just make sure you have a runny yolk. Set aside.

6. After you have removed the bacon, raise the oven heat to broil

7. Add burgers to a hot grill or large griddle on

high heat. Cook burgers 3-6 min on each side, depending on desired level of doneness. You want them about 80% of the way to your desired level of doneness; we'll be finishing them in the broiler. Tip: Flip *only once!* This ensures maximum juice retention.

8. Assemble your burgers on the broiler pan in the following order: Burger patty, garlic aioli, 2 crossed strips of bacon, egg, and cheese (if using). Broil 1-2 min, until cheese is melted. If not using cheese, this step may be skipped, so long as the burgers are already cooked to your desired temperature.

9. Add mustard, if desired and wrap the finished burger in lettuce. Serve with fried squash or sweet potato.

Yield: 4 half-pound burgers.

PALEO

CHICKEN

Chicken qualifies as comfort food in any home! It's one of those things that everybody loves (except vegetarians!), and it can be used in more ways that any other meat. Another way in which chicken comforts us is that it's *easy* to cook!

When it comes to the paleo diet, chicken carries some of the same requirements as beef. You want it organic, if possible, and pastured is best. Grain-fed, factory farmed chickens are pumped full of chemicals that not only rob the meat of it's natural beauty, but some of it's natural nutrition as well!

If you're buying quality bird, there's no doubt these recipes will be a hit in your home.

Slow-Roasted Chicken, The Right Way

There's something about a slow cooked chicken that just says *home*. That crispy skin, the fall-apart texture, it just can't be beat.

This recipe has a dose of herbs and aromatics that will make your kitchen smell amazing, and make your heart sing when you take that first bite.

Ingredients:

1 whole chicken, 4-6 lbs
1/4 cup grapeseed oil
Salt and pepper, to taste
1/2 onion
1/2 orange
1/2 lemon
2 sprigs fresh thyme
2 sprigs fresh rosemary
5-6 leaves fresh sage

Directions:

1. Clean any giblets out of the middle of the chicken. Save them for making

stock! Tip: *Do not* wash the outside of your chicken. The splashing water can spread bacteria all over your kitchen. Any bacteria will be thoroughly killed during cooking.

2. Preheat the oven to 350 degrees.

3. In a small mixing bowl, stir together the salt and pepper. If desired, chop up about half the herbs and mix them in as well.

4. Pour the oil over the chicken and rub to coat the entire bird. Rub in the seasoning mixture with your hands, ensuring that every part gets coated.

5. Place the orange, lemon, onion and fresh herbs in the cavity of the chicken. Place the chicken into a large baking dish.

6. Bake at 350 for 2- 2 1/2 hours, until skin is crispy and chicken is thoroughly cooked.

Yield: about 4 servings.

Asian Chicken Stir-Fry

Asian flavors go great on chicken, and when you add a heaping helping of the right vegetables, you've got yourself a meal that nobody can turn down!

This recipe calls for honey, which is one of those paleo gray areas. If you do not tolerate honey in your diet, simply omit it from this recipe.

Ingredients:

2 boneless, skinless chicken breasts, cut into thin strips
1/2 onion, sliced
1 red bell pepper, sliced
1 green bell pepper, sliced
2 cups broccoli crowns
1 cup mushrooms, sliced
1/4 cup sliced almonds, toasted (optional)
1/4 cup coconut oil, for frying
1/2 cup coconut aminos
1 tbsp sesame oil
2 cloves garlic, grated
2 tsp fresh ginger, grated
1/2 tsp crushed red pepper (optional)
1/8 tsp ground allspice

1/8 tsp ground nutmeg
1/8 tsp ground anise
1/4 cup raw, organic honey
Juice and zest of 1 lime
1/4 cup fresh cilantro, chopped

Directions:

1. In a wok or large skillet over high heat, melt the coconut oil.

2. Add the chicken, onions and peppers to the oil and fry for 3-4 min. Remove and drain on paper towels. Discard the oil.

3. Return the wok to the fire and reduce the heat to medium. Add the sesame oil, coconut aminos, garlic, ginger, red pepper, allspice, nutmeg, anise and honey. Whisk until everything is well combined.

4. Return chicken, peppers and onions to the wok. Add mushrooms and broccoli. Stir-fry for 4-5 min, until the chicken is thoroughly cooked and all the vegetables are slightly soft.

5. Add the almonds and stir-fry 1 additional minute.

6. Plate the stir-fry and garnish with lime juice, lime zest and cilantro. Serve with riced cauliflower, or just on it's own.

Yield: about 2 servings.

Asian Chicken Lettuce Cups

This lovely little appetizer is great to serve at parties, but it can also be a light, refreshing lunch or dinner at home! Complete with a nutty dipping sauce, this dish recreates one of everyone's restaurant favorites.

Ingredients:

2 boneless, skinless chicken breasts, cut into thin strips
1/2 onion, thinly sliced
2 tbsp coconut oil
1/4 cup coconut aminos
1/2 tsp fresh ginger, grated
1 clove garlic, grated
8-10 leaves butter lettuce
1/3 cup all-natural almond butter
1 tbsp sesame oil
3 tbsp rice vinegar
1 tbsp coconut aminos
1 tsp black pepper
1 tsp garlic powder
1/2 tsp ground ginger
1/2 tsp crushed red pepper (optional)

Directions:

1. In a small mixing bowl, whisk together the almond butter, 1 tbsp sesame oil, rice vinegar, 1 tbsp coconut aminos, black pepper, garlic powder, ground ginger and crushed red pepper. This is your dipping sauce.

2. Toss sliced chicken with 1 tsp sesame oil, 1/2 cup coconut aminos, fresh ginger and fresh garlic.

3. In a wok or large skillet, melt the coconut oil.

4. Add onions and sautee until slightly charred, about 3 min. Add chicken mixture and sautee until chicken is thoroughly cooked, about 5-8 min.

5. Arrange chicken and onions on lettuce leaves. Serve with almond sauce for dipping.

Yield: 8-10 lettuce cups.

Garlic Chicken Thighs

For those in the know, chicken thighs are the best part of the bird. They're fatty, which means they're flavorful, an they've got a good helping of skin that can be easily crisped up in the oven. Thank goodness these birds have junk in their trunk! This recipe is simple, but delicious, like all the best food out there, paleo or not!

Ingredients:

4 chicken thighs
6 cloves garlic, minced
2 tbsp olive oil
Salt and pepper, to taste
1/4 cup fresh parsley, chopped

Directions:

1. Preheat oven to 350 degrees. Preheat a large, oven-proof skillet over medium-high heat.

2. In a large mixing bowl, combine all ingredients. Toss until chicken is well coated.

3. Lay chicken in skillet skin-side down. Cook 5-7 min, until skin is nicely browned and beginning to get crispy.

4. Flip the thighs and transfer the skillet into the oven. Bake at 350 for 15-20 min, until chicken reaches an internal temperature of 165 or higher. Serve with sauteed vegetables or roasted turnips.

Yield: 4 servings.

Nut-Crusted Fried Chicken

Fried chicken is something that nobody can resist. That crispy outer layer just makes everything inside that much better. This recipe substitutes the flour for almond meal – something you should already have on hand if you've made almond milk. If not, it's available in most stores these days.

With an extra dose of nuts, this dish is crunchy enough to satisfy your wildest cravings. We used boneless breasts here, but this could easily be done with any part of the bird.

Ingredients:

4 boneless, skinless chicken breasts, pounded to 1/2" thick
1 cup almond meal
1/4 cup raw almonds
1/4 cup raw cashews
1/4 cup pecans
1/4 cup walnuts
2 tbsp fresh parsley, chopped
Salt and pepper, to taste
4 eggs
1/4 cup almond milk
Salt and pepper, to taste
Grapeseed oil, for frying

Directions:

1. Pat your chicken breasts very dry with a paper towel.

2. In a large baking dish, whisk together the eggs and almond milk. Season generously with salt and pepper.

3. In a food processor or blender, grind the nuts to a fine powder. Add to another large baking dish. Add almond meal and parsley. Season generously with salt and pepper.

4. Add enough oil to a large, heavy bottom skillet so that breasts will be half submerged. Heat over medium-high heat until oil reaches 350 degrees.

5. Dredge each chicken breast in egg mixture, then nut mixture. Shake off any excess, then transfer to hot oil. Fry until rich golden brown, about 6-8 min per side.

Yield: 4 servings.

Shredded Mexican Chicken

If you're looking for something south of the border, this handy little dish is perfect for you. It's easy enough to make on a week night, and satisfying enough to serve to guests at a dinner party.

Ingredients:

4 boneless, skinless chicken breasts
2 cups chicken stock
1 cup home-made salsa
1 tbsp ground cumin
1 tbsp chipotle chili powder
2 tsp dried oregano
salt and pepper, to taste
2 tbsp olive oil
1/2 onion, thinly sliced
1 red bell pepper, thinly sliced
1 green bell pepper, thinly sliced
2 jalapenos, halved

Directions:

1. In a large, heavy bottom skillet over high heat, heat the oil. Sautee the peppers and

139

onions until slightly charred.

2. Add all ingredients to a crock pot. Alternatively, preheat the oven to 300 and add all ingredients to a dutch oven.

3. Allow to cook in the crock pot on high for 1 hour. Reduce heat to low and cook an additional 6-8 hours. If using a dutch oven, 3 hours at 300 is sufficient.

4. Remove chicken and shred with a fork. Chicken should shred easily.

5. Top with peppers and onions and a drizzle of the broth. Add cilantro, lime juice and avocado, if desired.

PALEO

PORK

Pork has got to be one of the more hotly disputed meats in the butcher's case. Some people are nuts for it, some people just don't like it, some people don't cook it because they're afraid to *undercook* it, many people consider it too fattening, its even against some people's religion!

Whatever your personal feeling on pork, it deserves an honored place in the paleo kitchen. Pork fat is one of the best cooking oils you can use, and the meat itself can be served in so many ways it's worth exploring, even if you're not used to having it in your diet. When prepared right, it can be the ultimate comfort food.

In this chapter we'll go over a handful of ways to cook pork. Each recipe can easily be expanded upon to create a new level of flavor each time you cook it. Presented here are some of the basic (and tastiest!) methods to cook this delicious meat.

Carnitas

Carnitas is that classic Mexican dish that pork lovers go nuts for. It's kind of like pulled pork, Mexican style; slow cooked, fall-apart texture, bold spicy flavor, everything a good piece of pork should be. This recipe shows you how to make the classic recipe paleo-style.

Ingredients:

2-4 pounds bone-in pork shoulder
3 cups water
1/2 onion
1 orange, halved, no seeds if possible
2 jalapenos, halved
2 tbsp grapeseed oil
4 cloves garlic
2 bay leaves
2 tbsp coconut milk
1 tsp ground oregano
1 tbsp salt
1 tbsp black pepper
1 cinnamon stick
3-4 whole allspice pods
1 tsp ground cumin
1 tsp chipotle chili powder

Directions:

1. Preheat the oven to 300 degrees.

2. Heat the dutch oven over high heat. Add the grapeseed oil, onions, garlic and jalapenos. Allow to cook on one side for 6-7 min, until thoroughly charred. Remove from pan.

3. Season the pork liberally with salt and pepper. Add to dutch oven and sear on all sides, 1-2 min per side.

4. Add vegetable back to dutch oven. Add the water and bring to a simmer. Water should come about three quarters of the way up the meat. Use more or less as needed.

5. Add all herbs, spices and seasonings. Squeeze as much juice as possible out of the orange halves and add them to the broth. Add coconut milk.

6. Cover and transfer dutch oven to the preheated oven and cook for 2 hours, until pork is fall apart tender and the bone slips right out. Shred and top with avocado and homemade salsa.

Yield: about 4-6 servings.

Spinach Stuffed Pork Chops

A stuffed pork chop is a small culinary achievement that will make you feel like a giant in the kitchen. It's not all that hard to do, it just takes a little time, but once you serve it to guests or family, you'll be soaking in the praise for your beautiful, delicious dish.

Pork is often stuffed with cheese or dairy products, but since we're *mostly* keeping things dairy free, we presented this one with a simple spinach filling and an almond meal crust that you're going to love.

Ingredients:

1 whole boneless pork loin, 2-4 pounds
1/2 cup ghee, divided
8-10 cups raw spinach, thoroughly rinsed, stems removed
2 cloves garlic, minced
Juice and zest of 1 lemon
Salt and pepper, to taste
1 cup almond meal
1/2 cup paleo mayo
1 tsp paprika
1/2 tsp ground sage

1/2 tsp dried oregano
Salt and pepper, to taste

Directions:

1. Preheat the oven to 350 degrees.

2. With a long, very sharp knife, cut about an inch into the pork loin lengthwise. Pull the resulting flap away and cut diagonally into the loin, rolling as you do. The idea is to cut the pork loin into a sheet about 1/2" to 1" thick that can be rolled up like a cake roll or a yule log. If you need detailed instructions, search for videos online. You can also ask your butcher to do it for you.

3. In a large skillet over medium heat, melt 2 tbsp of the ghee.

4. Add the spinach, garlic, lemon zest and lemon juice. Sautee until spinach is just wilted. Season lightly with salt and pepper. Allow spinach to cool 5-10 min.

5. Spread the remaining ghee onto the interior surface of the pork loin. Season with salt and pepper, and top with cooled spinach mixture.

6. Roll the loin back up on itself, just as you would with a cake roll or yule log.

7. Place the loin in a large baking dish with high sides.

8. In a small mixing bowl, stir together the mayo, almond meal, paprika, sage and oregano. Season with salt and pepper.

9. Spread almond meal mixture over the top of the loin. Do not spread down the sides, just on the top.

10. Bake at 350 for 1 hour, 30 minutes, or until the roast reaches an internal temperature of 165 degrees.

11. Slice into chops and serve.

Yield: 4-8 servings.

Grilled, Smoked Pork Tenderloin

Pork tenderloin, like beef tenderloin, is a prized cut of meat. It has many of the same qualities – intense tenderness, rich flavor, low fat content – but it also has something its beef counterpart doesn't. It's dirt cheap!

This yummy cut of meat is cheap enough to eat a couple times a week, if you like it. We hope this recipe convinces you that you should.

Ingredients:

1-2 pounds pork tenderloin
1 recipe mustard marinade (check out chapter 3!)
2 cups dry wood chips

Directions:

1. Marinate the pork in the marinade for up to 2 days. It's tender enough on it's own, but the mustard flavor penetrates deep and brings this dish to life.

2. When meat is marinated, wrap the wood chips in foil and poke several holes in the

foil.

3. Turn on one side of the grill only, or if using charcoals, move all coals to one side of the grill.

4. Place a pan of water under the cool side of the grill.

5. Place the wood chips over the heat. Turn heat to high and cover the grill. When it starts smoking, reduce heat to lowest setting and place pork over the cool side of the grill.

6. Grill 30-40 min, turning once, until internal temperature reaches 165 degrees. Remove from heat immediately, and allow to rest 10 minutes before slicing.

Yield: 2-4 servings

BBQ Pulled Pork, The Easy Way

Maybe you don't have a smoker. Maybe the smoking technique outlined in the previous recipe is still more work than you have time for. That doesn't mean you can't make brilliant BBQ pork at home.

Braising is one of those cooking methods that makes food so delicious it seems hard, but anyone who has braised a piece of meat will tell you how easy it is. All you do is throw everything in the pot and let it cook! This recipe takes one of our favorite spice mixes and turns it into a dish that nobody will turn down.

Ingredients:

1 recipe BBQ spice rub (check out ours in chapter 2)
2-4 pounds bone-in pork shoulder
2 cups chicken stock
1 cup apple juice
2 tbsp ghee or animal fat
1 onion, quartered
4 cloves garlic

Directions:

1. Preheat the oven to 300 degrees.

2. Rub about half the spice rub onto the outside of the pork shoulder. Allow to rest for 10 minutes at room temperature.

3. In a dutch oven, melt the ghee or animal fat. Add onions and garlic, sautee 6-8 min until onions are nicely charred.

4. Add pork to dutch oven, sear on all sides, about 1-2 min per side.

5. Deglaze pan with apple juice. Bring to a simmer.

6. Add chicken stock and remaining seasoning mix.

7. Cover and transfer dutch oven to the preheated oven. Cook at 300 for 2 hours, until pork is fall-apart tender and bone slips out easily. Serve with paleo-friendly BBQ sauce.

Yield: 4-8 servings.

Braised BBQ Ribs

Traditionally, true BBQ flavor is achieved by several hours or even days in a smoker. This isn't always easy to pull of at home, since most of us don't have the right equipment. But with a little ingenuity, you can pull off deep, bold BBQ flavor at home.

This recipe combines the techniques from the previous two recipes to create a rack of ribs that would hold its own at any BBQ competition.

Ingredients:

1 recipe BBQ spice rub (check out ours in chapter 2)
1-2 racks of pork spare ribs
2 cups chicken stock
1 cup apple juice
2 tbsp ghee or animal fat
1 onion, quartered
4 cloves garlic
2 cups dry wood chips
Additional BBQ seasoning mix

Directions:

1. Preheat the oven to 300 degrees.

2. Remove silverskin from ribs. Rub about half the spice rub onto the outside of the ribs. Allow to rest for 10 minutes at room temperature.

3. In a dutch oven, melt the ghee or animal fat. Add onions and garlic, sautee 6-8 min until onions are nicely charred.

4. Add apple juice, chicken stock, and remaining seasoning mix. Bring to a rolling boil.

5. Add ribs. Cover and transfer the dutch oven to the preheated oven and cook for 1 hour, until ribs are cooked, but not quite falling apart.

6. Remove the ribs from the dutch oven. Allow to cool for 10 min.

7. Preheat the grill to low heat.

8. Season ribs with additional BBQ seasoning mix, or brush with paleo-friendly BBQ sauce. Grill over low heat 5-10 min, then raise heat to high and grill an additional 5

min until ribs are lightly charred and tender. Serve with sauce for dipping.

Yield: 2-4 servings.

"Breaded" Pork Tenderloin

If you've ever been to a county fair, chances are you've seen them: the ridiculously large breaded pork tenderloin sandwiches that extend a good 4-5 inches out of the bun. Well that's what this recipe is all about.

The bun may be out, but there's still something alluring about a crispy-fried, pounded thin piece of pork that we can't resist. If you tolerate cheese in your paleo diet, you might also try topping these with a slice of melted cheddar.

Ingredients:

1-2 pork tenderloins
1/4 cup apple cider vinegar
1-2 cups water
1/4 cup salt
1 tbsp pepper
4-6 eggs
1/4 cup almond milk
1 1/2 cups almond meal
Salt and pepper, to taste
Grapeseed oil, for frying

Directions:

1. In a large resealable container, combine the cider vinegar and salt. Place the tenderloins in this mixture and fill with enough water to cover. Shake to mix brine together.

2. Allow pork to brine 4 hours, up to 2 days.

3. Remove pork from brine and pat dry with a paper towel. Pound to 1/2" thick with a meat mallet.

4. In a deep fryer or a large, heavy bottom skillet, heat enough oil to completely submerge one large tenderloin. Heat oil to 350 degrees.

5. In a shallow baking dish, whisk together almond milk and eggs. Season liberally with salt and pepper.

6. In a similar baking dish, season almond meal with salt and pepper and whisk to combine.

7. One at a time, dredge flattened pork in the egg wash, then the almond meal. Fry in oil until golden brown on both sides, about 20 min total. Serve with paleo mayo for dipping.

Yield: 2-4 servings.

PALEO

SEAFOOD

The amazing thing about seafood is just how low in calories it is, considering how amazing it tastes. As a protein-fueled paleo person, mountains of seafood aren't out of the question!

Seafood can be on the expensive side, depending on your tastes, but it can also be one of the greatest ways to show your culinary skills.

Most seafood has a delicate, one-of-a-kind flavor that can easily be overpowered by over-seasoning, overcooking or worst of all over-fussing. If you take one lesson away from this chapter, let it be this: if in doubt, wait it out. The main challenge of seafood is cooking it for *exactly* the right amount of time. Too little, it could fall apart on you and even be dangerous. Too much, and it all winds up tasting like canned tuna.

Here we won't delve into anything too difficult, but make sure you watch everything closely. After a few tries, you'll be a master.

Grilled Mahi-Mahi Kabobs

Mahi-Mahi is a delicious, meaty-textured whitefish that can actually stand up to grilling, when treated properly. Served on a skewer with some seasoned veggies, it's the perfect dish for cooking out on a summer's eve.

Ingredients:

4 filets (6-8 oz) Mahi-Mahi, cut into 3/4" pieces
1/4 cup olive oil
1/4 cup ghee, melted
2 tbsp fresh parsley, chopped
2 tbsp fresh cilantro, chopped
2 cloves garlic, minced
Juice and zest of 1 lemon
2 tsp pepper
1 tsp salt
2 large yellow squash, sliced
2 large zucchini, sliced
1 onion, quartered

Directions:

1. In a small mixing bowl, combine olive oil, ghee, parsley, cilantro, garlic, lemon juice,

lemon zest, pepper and salt. Whisk to combine.

2. Add the fish and the vegetables to a large mixing bowl, and drizzle with about 2/3 of the oil mixture. Toss to coat evenly.

3. Arrange vegetables and fish onto skewers.

4. Brush the grill grate with oil and preheat to high heat.

5. Grill the kabobs 2-3 min on each side, until fish is flaky and vegetables are slightly charred. Serve with guacamole for dipping.

Yield: about 4 servings.

Spicy Cajun Shrimp

Ingredients:

1 pound shrimp, deveined, shell on
1 recipe Cajun spice mix (see chapter 2)
1/2 onion
2 cloves garlic
1/2 cup ghee, divided

Directions:

1. In medium saucepan, bring 2 cups of water to a boil. Add 1/4 cup ghee, about 3/4 of the spice mix, the onion and the garlic. Return to a rolling boil.

2. Add shrimp and boil until pink, about 5-7 min.

3. Remove shrimp from broth and allow to cool for 5 min. Sprinkle shrimp with remaining spice mixture.

4. Melt the other 1/4 cup butter and serve as a dipping sauce.

Yield: about 2 servings.

Tuna Tartare

Tuna Tartare is an incredible way to eat fresh fish. If the idea of raw fish turns you off, this dish might just change your mind.

Raw meats are not considered safe to eat largely because of the processing that goes into getting them ready for sale. This is especially true of fish, as it is most often frozen and shipped long distances. The truth is, however, that as long as they've never been frozen, most fish and some meats are quite safe (and delicious!) raw. Tuna is perhaps the best recognized of these.

If you don't like fishy flavor, then raw tuna is the fish for you. The fishy flavor is a result of overcooking and over processing. When served raw, tuna has a light, delicious flavor that you are guaranteed to enjoy.

Ingredients:

1 pound fresh (never frozen) tuna steak
1/4 cup olive oil
Juice and zest of 1 lime
1 tsp fresh grated horseradish
1 tsp mustard

1 tbsp coconut aminos
1 tsp crushed red pepper
2 tsp salt
1 tsp pepper
2 green onions, minced
1/2 jalapeno, ribs and seeds removed, diced
1 avocado, diced
2 tsp toasted sesame seeds

Directions:

1. Dice the tuna steak into 1/4" cubes and place in a medium mixing bowl.

2. In a separate mixing bowl, whisk together oil, lime juice, lime zest, horseradish, mustard, coconut aminos, crushed red pepper, salt and pepper.

3. Pour sauce over tuna. Add green onions, jalapeno and sesame seeds. Mix well.

4. Add the avocado and gently fold it in, making sure not to crush it into guacamole.

5. Allow the tartare to chill in the refrigerator for 1 hour before serving. Serve with sliced fresh vegetables for dipping.

Yield: 5-6 servings.

Paleo Crab Cakes

Crab cakes without breadcrumbs? Blasphemy! Or is it?

If this is the first recipe you've turned to in this book, you may not know that virtually anything that can be done with flour or breadcrumbs can be made paleo with a few clever tricks. Crab cakes are no exception. The best news of all is that (as with many paleo recipes) once you make the substitution, the resulting dish is all about the meat. Which is the way it should have been all along.

Ingredients:

1 pound cooked crab meat
1/4 onion, minced
3 tbsp paleo mayo
1 clove garlic, minced
salt and pepper to taste
1/4 tsp chipotle chili powder
1 egg
2-3 tbsp tapioca flour (as needed to make mixture stick)
1/4 cup grapeseed oil

Directions:

1. Add crab, onion, mayo, garlic, salt, pepper, chili powder and egg to a large mixing bowl and mix well with your hands.

2. Add tapioca flour 1 tbsp at a time until mixture sticks together.

3. In a large, heavy bottom skillet, heat grapeseed oil over medium-high heat.

4. Form crab mixture into patties of the desired size. Fry 2-3 min on each side. Serve with a drizzle of red pepper aioli.

Yield: about 4 servings.

Blackened Salmon

This one is a no-brainer. Blackened salmon is one of the best pieces of fish you can eat, that's why you see it everywhere. And it's seriously easy to make. Almost too easy to write a recipe for it. But we've included one any way, just to we can go over the proper technique of cooking fish filets. No more shredded fish in your house!

Ingredients:

4 filets salmon (6-8 oz each)
1 recipe Cajun seasoning mix (check it out in chapter 2)
1/4 cup olive oil, divided
1/2 cup paleo mayo
Juice and zest of 1/2 lemon
2 tbsp dill pickles, minced
1/4 tsp dill
1/4 tsp black pepper

Directions:

1. In a small mixing bowl, combine the mayo, lemon juice, lemon zest, minced pickle, dill and pepper. This is your home made tartar

sauce.

2. Preheat a grill or large skillet over medium-high heat. Oil the grill grate, or place 2 tsbp of the oil in a skillet.

3. Gently rub the outside of your salmon with olive oil. Season generously with seasoning mix.

4. Place your salmon on the grill or skillet. If you have skin on your salmon, start skin side down.

5. Cook 3-4 min. The fish will tell you when it's ready to flip. If you stick a spatula under it and it doesn't want to release, wait. Try again in 30-45 seconds. When it is ready to flip, it should come off without shredding apart.

6. If working with a skillet, you may also preheat the oven to 350 degrees and transfer the skillet to the oven for 5-8 minutes after flipping the fish. This is a great, gentle way to cook it.

7. Either way, cook the second side about as long as you cooked the first side and your fish will be perfectly done. Trust the process and don't mess with it too much!

8. Serve with a dollop of the homemade tartar sauce.

Yield: 4 servings.

Grilled Fish "Tacos"

There are recipes out there for paleo tortillas, but the result is usually a little eggy and disappointing. If you are really craving tacos, they might remind you of a tortilla just enough to get you by, but we feel that all you really need is the cooling crisp of fresh lettuce. Especially with fish tacos.

The delicate flavor of taco-seasoned fish isn't something you should overpower with flavor packed tortillas or huge dollops of salsa. It should be able to shine through, and the condiments should compliment it, not drown it out. Submitted here is our method for achieving exactly this.

Ingredients:

4 filets tilapia or other white fish (6-8 oz each)
1/4 cup olive oil, plus more for the grill
1 recipe taco seasoning (you'll find it back in chapter 2)
8 large leaves butter or iceberg lettuce
1/2 cup homemade salsa (find that one in chapter 4)
1 avocado, diced
lime juice, to garnish
1/4 cup fresh cilantro, chopped

Directions:

1. Preheat the grill to high heat. Oil the grate with olive oil.

2. Gently rub your fish filets with olive oil and season lightly with taco seasoning mix.

3. Grill the fish 3-4 min on each side, flipping only when the fish is ready to release. If you stick a spatula under it and the fish doesn't want to come, leave it alone. Check again in 30-45 seconds.

4. When your fish filets are done, remove them from the heat and cut each one in half lengthwise.

5. Arrange the fish on the lettuce leaves. Top with a small drizzle of salsa, a few cubes of avocado, a spritz of lime juice and s sprinkle of cilantro. Wrap and enjoy!

Yield: 8 tacos, about 2-4 servings.

PALEO

SIDE DISHES

You may have noticed by now that none of our entree dishes came with pre-matched accompaniments. While every dish has it's perfect pairing, we thought it would be best to break things down a bit and present you several chapters of shorter, simpler recipes. That way, you can mix and match yourself without having to read half of one recipe and half of another!

Most of these sides will go good with anything, and if you're a paleo vegetarian, you'll probably find a lot to work with here. Hopefully, this chapter will contain something for everyone, and something to fit every dish we've outlined in the previous chapters.

Brussels Sprouts with Pine Nuts and Lardons

Brussels sprouts are a pleasure one usually has to grow into. As kids we see adults eating the weird-looking little balls, we smell the aroma they put off and we decide they're not for us. Flash forward twenty years or so, however, and we're gobbling them down like there's no tomorrow.

These little sprouts are not only delicious, they're also packed with nutrition. This recipe adds a little pork to the equation to make sure it's enticing enough for the whole family.

Ingredients:

1 pound Brussels sprouts, cleaned and quartered
1/4 cup pine nuts, toasted
1/2 pound uncured pork belly or paleo-friendly, nitrate-free bacon, cut into pieces
1/4 onion, diced
2 tbsp olive oil
Salt and pepper, to taste

Directions:

1. Toast the pine nuts by shaking them around in a dry pan for 4-5 min.

2. In a large skillet, warm the olive oil, over medium-high heat.

3. Add pork, sautee until almost crispy about 5-8 min.

4. Add onions, sautee 3-4 more min.

5. Add Brussels sprouts. Allow to cook on one side 2-3 min, until lightly charred, then cover with a lid and allow to steam 5 min, until cooked through.

6. Remove lid and continue to cook an additional 3-5 min, if you like them charred. Serve hot.

Yield: about 4 servings.

Mashed Cauliflower

Let's be honest. Every paleo eater misses potatoes once in a while. But after you try this dish, you'll start to wonder why.

Anything a potato can do, there's another vegetable that can do it healthier and tastier. Cauliflower is the champ when it comes to recreating a loaded mashed potato, and that's exactly what this recipe lets you do.

Ingredients:

1 head cauliflower, cut into crowns
1/4 pound uncured pork belly or paleo-friendly, nitrate-free bacon, cut into pieces
2 tbsp ghee
1 tbsp coconut milk
1 tbsp almond milk
2 green onions, chopped
1/2 cup shredded cheese (if tolerated)
Salt & pepper to taste

Directions:

1. Place the cauliflower in a large saucepan

and cover with water. Salt the water and bring to a boil over high heat. Boil for 15 minutes.

2. While the cauliflower boils, put the pork pieces in a skillet over medium-high heat and sautee until crispy. Allow to drain on paper towels.

3. Drain the cauliflower and transfer it to a large mixing bowl. Add pork, ghee, coconut milk, almond milk, green onions, and cheese (if using). Season to taste with salt and pepper.

4. Mash with a potato masher or a pastry cutter until mixture is thick, about the consistency of mashed potatoes. Serve hot.

Yield: 4 servings.

Cauliflower "Rice"

Rice is another one of those things that paleo people *think* they miss, but the truth is they just haven't found the right substitute yet. This cauli rice has a mild enough flavor to go with a variety of dishes. The only way in which it doesn't stand up to rice is that it doesn't keep particularly well. The solution? Eat it hot off the stove! No problem, right?

Ingredients:

1 head cauliflower
2 tbsp ghee
Salt and pepper to taste.

Directions:

1. If you have a food processor with a shredder attachment, simply shred the cauliflower this way. If not, grate the cauliflower with a cheese grater. Season with salt and pepper, or other flavors, if desired. Coconut aminos and sesame oil make a great Asian-inspired combo; salsa and ground cumin make good Mexican rice.

2. Melt the ghee in a large skillet over medium-high heat.

3. Add the cauliflower and a few tablespoons of water. Cover and cook for 3 min, then uncover and cook, stirring frequently 1 additional minute. Serve as you would normal rice.

Yield: 4 servings.

Oven Roasted Turnips and Beets

Beets are an acquired taste, but to those who *have* acquired it, there's no root veggie better. The distinct bitter, aromatic flavor is not to be found in the rest of the produce aisle.

If you buy fresh beets (not the awful canned stuff) one of the best ways to serve them is simply roasted in the oven. It's a great comfort food, and goes well anywhere you would put a roasted potato. Turnips, with their milder, radish-esque flavor, round out this dish for a side that goes well with steak, roasted chicken or just on it's own.

Ingredients:

3-4 large beets, tops removed, peeled and quartered
3-4 large turnips, peeled and quartered
2 cloves garlic, minced
1/2 onion, minced
1/4 cup olive oil
2 tbsp fresh parsley, chopped
1 tbsp fresh rosemary, chopped
1 tbsp fresh thyme, chopped
salt and pepper to taste

Directions:

1. Preheat the oven to 400 degrees.

2. In a large mixing bowl, toss all ingredients together until beets and turnips are well coated.

3. Transfer to a 9" x 13" baking dish. Bake at 400 degrees 12-15 min, until a fork slides easily into the flesh of a beet. Serve as you would roasted potatoes.

Yield: 6-8 servings

Sweet Potato Fries

Sweet potatoes or yams are a great addition to your paleo diet, and while they taste great baked with a little ghee and ground cinnamon, there's really no good reason we can't fry them up to go alongside out next paleo burger. As long as the oil is right, you can fry to your heart's content!

Ingredients:

2 large sweet potatoes, peeled and cut into thin fries
Grapeseed oil, for frying
Salt and pepper, to taste

Directions:

1. In a deep fryer or a large stock pot, heat the oil to 350 degrees. Reduce heat slightly if needed to maintain this temperature.

2. Working in batches, fry sweet potatoes 4-5 min, until browned at edges. Remove from oil and allow to drain on paper towels.

3. Allow fries to cool all the way to room

181

temperature.

4. Reheat the oil and, working in batches, fry again 4-5 min, until fries float on top of the oil and are nicely browned.

5. Remove from fryer, sprinkle with salt and pepper immediately and drain on paper towels. Serve hot with a mix of mayo and mustard for dipping.

Yield: 4 servings.

Baked Cajun Butternut Fries

If frying isn't your thing, this little baked fry recipe is just the thing you need to get that perfect burger accompaniment without all the fuss and mess of frying. Butternut squash is starchy enough to act like a potato in most settings, yet has a unique, buttery flavor that is perfectly accented by a dash of Cajun seasoning. Baked in the oven, they're a no-mess French fry that everyone will love.

Ingredients:

1 large butternut squash, peeled, seeded and cut into fries
1/4 cup grapeseed oil
Cajun seasoning (check it out in chapter 2), as needed

Directions:

1. Preheat oven to 375 degrees. Grease 2 large sheet pans with grapeseed oil

2. In a large mixing bowl, toss the fries with the grapeseed oil until well coated. Add a little of the seasoning mix at a time and toss until evenly distributed. Don't use too

much, just enough to give the fries a light coat.

3. Arrange the fries on the sheet pans and bake at 375 for 15-20 min, turning the fries once during cooking. Serve with your choice of paleo dipping sauces.

Yield: 3-4 servings.

Veggie Chips

Like we've said; anything a potato can do, there's a veggie that can do it better. You've seen these, they're the fancy, multicolored veggie chips that come in those dark, gourmet-looking bags. Yep, you can make those at home too. It's not even hard.

This recipe uses a method for making these chips that produces a longer, thinner chip. You could easily shave the veggies with a mandoline if you prefer a broader chip.

Ingredients:

1 large turnip, peeled
1 large yam, peeled
1 large red beet, peeled
1 large rutabega, peeled
2-3 large carrots, peeled
2-3 large parsnips, peeled
Grapeseed oil, for frying
Salt and pepper, to taste

Directions:

1. In a deep fryer or large stock pot, heat the oil to 350 degrees.

2. Use a carrot peeler to shave large sections of each vegetable into a large mixing bowl. Press hard to get an ideal thickness. If you want, you can even shave the pieces in random patterns to make a beautiful twirly chip.

3. Fry the chips in batches of about 1 cup, until chips are browned and crispy. Season with salt and pepper and drain on paper towels.

Yield: about 8-10 servings.

Veggie Latkes

Here's another in a line of recipes that shows you that potatoes ain't got nothin' on the rest of the root veggie world. These latkes can be made with *any* starchy root veggie or any kind of squash. Some may brown a little more or less than others, but all taste just as great alongside any paleo entree.

Ingredients:

2 small zucchini
2 large parsnips, peeled
2 large carrots, peeled
1 medium turnip, peeled
2 eggs, beaten
salt and pepper to taste
Grapeseed oil, for frying

Directions:

1. Using the shredder attachment of a food processor, or a cheese grater, shred the vegetables. Pat dry with paper towels. The more moisture you absorb, the better texture the latkes will have.

2. Season with salt and pepper and add the eggs. Mix with your hands until everything is evenly distributed.

3. In a large, heavy bottom skillet, heat about 1/2" of grapeseed oil to 350 degrees.

4. Grab a handful of the vegetable mixture and form it into a 1 1/2" patty with your hands. Toss it in the oil. Repeat until skillet is full.

5. Fry each latke about 3-5 min, then flip and fry an additional 3-5 min on the other side.

6. Remove from oil, season with salt and pepper and drain on paper towels. Serve hot with paleo dipping sauces.

Yield: 3-4 servings.

Grilled Artichokes

These make a great party appetizer, or just something for the family to munch on while you wrap up the rest of dinner. They might take a time or two to master; the texture is a bit fickle with artichokes. But no matter what, you always end up with a delicious heart that will be enough to keep you trying.

Ingredients:

1 large artichoke
½ cup lemon juice, divided
2 tbsp balsamic vinegar
2 tbsp olive or grapeseed oil
1 tsp garlic powder
salt and pepper to taste
Balsamic mayo for dipping (check out the recipe in chapter 4!)

Directions:

1. Cut the top 1/3 of the artichoke off. You'll know you cut enough if you can see some of the purple inner leaves. Using a pair of scissors, snip the sharp tips off the remaining leaves

2. Fill a large bowl with cold water and ¼ cup of the lemon juice. Bathe the cleaned artichoke in the lemon water, squeezing it to make sure water gets deep inside.

3. Fill a large pot with fresh water (do not re-use the water you cleaned it in) and the remaining ¼ cup lemon juice. Boil the artichoke on high heat for 30 minutes. Remove the artichoke from the water and allow to cool about 10 min.

4. Slice the artichoke in half and clean out the inner fuzz and purple leaves using a spoon to scoop them out.

5. Preheat the grill to high heat.

6. In a small mixing bowl, whisk together the oil, balsamic vinegar, garlic powder, salt and pepper. Baste some the mixture onto all sides of the artichoke using a brush.

7. Grill each side about 5 minutes over high heat. Baste with oil/vinegar mixture several times during cooking. Serve with balsamic mayo for dipping. Leaves should pluck right off. Eat by scraping the inner meat off of them using your teeth. Dip each leaf in a little mayo for extra flavor! Serve hot or cold. *Yield: 3-4 servings*

Green Bean Grill Pack

Paleo people are big grillers; after all when you eat a lot of meat and veggies, what better way is there to prepare food?

The grill pack is a mighty method for turning veggies that normally wouldn't work onto the grill into flavorful masterpieces. This recipe, however, is the benchmark by which all others should be judged.

Ingredients:

4 cups of fresh green beans, trimmed.
1/2 onion
4 strips paleo-friendly, uncured bacon
1/4 cup olive oil
salt and pepper, to taste

Directions:

1. Lay out a very large sheet of broad foil on the counter. 18" x 24" is ideal.

2. Take the 1/2 onion and cut it in half again. Separate the layers and lay half of them on

the foil. Season with salt and pepper and drizzle with oil.

3. Cut the bacon strips in half. Lay half of them over the onions. Season with salt and pepper.

4. Add the green beans to a large mixing bowl. Season heavily with salt and pepper and drizzle with olive oil. Place them atop the bacon and form into a rough rectangle.

5. Top with more bacon, season with more salt & pepper.

6. Top with more onions, season with more salt and pepper and a final drizzle of oil.

7. Fold two edges of the foil together and roll tight. Crimp in the sides to make a little pillow.

8. Preheat the grill to high heat.

9. Grill the foil package for 20 min on each side. Onions will be charred, bacon will be almost crisp and green beans will be nicely steamed. Serve with steaks for the perfect paleo meal.

Yield: about 4 servings.

Squash Grill Pack

Here's another foil-packed recipe that goes great with anything you're putting on the grill. This one even travels well; it's just as good cold!

Ingredients:

2 large zucchini, sliced thick
2 large yellow squash, sliced thick
1 onion, quartered
1 1/2 cups mushrooms, quartered
1/4 cup olive oil
1/4 cup fresh parsley, chopped
2 cloves garlic, minced
salt and pepper to taste

Directions:

1. Add all ingredients to a large mixing bowl and toss to coat. Make sure everything is evenly distributed.

2. Roll out a very large sheet of broad foil. 18" x 24" is ideal.

3. Pour the vegetables into the middle of the

foil. Pull two edges together and roll tight. Crimp in sides to form a little pillow.

4. Preheat a grill to high heat.

5. Grill 40 min, turning occasionally. Serve with pork tenderloin or paleo burgers.

Yield: about 4 servings.

PALEO

BREAKFAST

You can't talk about comfort food without talking about breakfast! There's nothing more comforting than a big, satisfying breakfast, and as paleo eaters, that's the only kind we have!

Paleo breakfasts rely heavily on eggs and meat – two things many people deny themselves at breakfast time. As a result, we go through our days full and fueled, which helps us make better decisions all day long.

The recipes in this chapter will show you just how wide the world of eggs and meat can be, if you're willing to put in a little time and effort. Pretty soon the idea of cereal and milk will be about as attractive as hardtack and gruel.

Tapioca Crepes with Berry Compote

This delectable little recipe gets you about as close to a crepe as a paleo chef can get. Don't call it a crepe in front of any French people, you might get slapped. But for unpretentious paleo eaters with the appetite of a cave man, these babies have everything a crepe has and more.

Ingredients:

1 cup tapioca flour
1 1/2 tsp baking powder
½ cup warm water
½ cup almond milk
4 eggs
pinch of salt
Ghee for the pan
2 cups fresh berries of your choice

Directions:

1. In a medium mixing bowl, whisk together the tapioca, coconut, baking powder, soda and salt.

2. In a large mixing bowl, whisk together the

eggs, water and coconut milk.

3. Mix the dry ingredients into the wet. Whisk vigorously until there are very few lumps. Batter will be runny.

4. In a small saucepan over medium heat, combine the berries with about 2 tbsp water. Allow to cook 5-6 min covered, stir, then remove from heat.

5. In a large heavy bottom skillet, melt the ghee.

6. Spoon about 1/4 cup of the batter into the hot pan at a time. Tilt the pan to spread it evenly. Cook 1-2 min, until the edges curl and the crepe comes loose when the pan is shaken. Flip, and cook an additional 30 seconds to 1 min on the other side. Repeat until all batter is used.

7. Place a small amount of the berries in the center of each crepe and fold in half, then in half again. Top with more berries, if desired.

Yield: 3-4 servings.

Sweet Potato Pancakes

This is a great hearty breakfast that tastes amazing after a long night. It takes a little extra time to whip up in the morning, but it's worth it to feel full and satisfied all the way to lunch.

We use shredded coconut to round out the flavor and just enough tapioca to get all the goodness to stick together. It's a meal you'll want to make every Saturday morning!

Ingredients:

1 large sweet potato, fully cooked and mashed
1/4 cup unsweetened shredded coconut
1/4 cup tapioca flour
2 eggs
1/2 cup coconut milk
1/4 cup almond milk
1/2 tsp cinnamon
1/8 tsp nutmeg
1 pinch salt
Ghee, for pan

Directions:

1. In a large mixing bowl, whisk together the sweet potato, coconut, tapioca flour, eggs, coconut milk, almond milk, cinnamon, nutmeg and salt. Whisk until smooth. Batter will be thicker than ordinary pancake batter.

2. Melt the ghee in a large heavy bottom skillet over medium-high heat.

3. Spoon about 1/4 cup of the batter into the pan. Spread with the spoon if batter is very thick.

4. Cook 3-4 min, until edges are golden brown. When the pancake is ready to flip, it will release from the pan easily without falling apart. If the pancake does not release, allow it to cook a few seconds longer.

5. Repeat until all batter is used.

6. Serve with eggs, or a drizzle of organic honey, if tolerated.

Yield: 3-4 servings.

Homemade Breakfast Sausage

Pork breakfast sausage is a super-hearty addition to any good breakfast, but unfortunately the stuff you can buy at the store is laden with sugar, nitrates and other nasty additives. It's just no good.

The thing is, breakfast sausage is just spiced pork. In the old days it wasn't full of icky junk, so why does it have to be today? Why can't we just whip it up the way we like it at home?

Well... We can.

Ingredients:

1 pound ground pork
1 tbsp salt
2 tsp pepper
1 tsp ground sage
1 tsp dried thyme
1/2 tsp ground rosemary
1/2 tsp paprika
1/2 tsp paprika
1/4 tsp ground cinnamon
1/4 tsp ground nutmeg
2 tsp raw, organic honey (if tolerated)

Directions:

1. In a large mixing bowl, combine all ingredients. Mix with your hands until everything is just distributed. Do not over work the meat.

2. Shape into patties or links and fry until fully cooked, about 3-5 min per side depending on the size of the patty. Serve with eggs or whatever else you like for breakfast.

3. Store any uncooked sausage in a vacuum-packed container, if possible. If not, store in a zip-top bag with as much air removed as possible. Flavors will develop in the refrigerator.

Yield: 1 pound sausage, about 4-6 servings.

Cheesy Egg Muffins

If you're looking to pre-cook something that you can grab on those busy mornings, this recipe is the perfect thing for you. They're quick enough to whip up at a moment's notice, and they keep a good 3-4 days in the refrigerator. Oh, and did we mention they're delicious?

This recipe calls for cheese, which is a gray area for some paleo eaters. These muffins cook up great without it, however if you're a purist. Add some uncured bacon or sausage for an extra boost of flavor.

Ingredients:

4 eggs
2 tbsp rendered animal fat
3 tbsp tapioca flour
1/2 tsp baking powder
8 oz shredded cheese (if tolerated)
Olive or grapeseed oil, to grease pan.

Directions:

1. Preheat oven to 375 degrees.

2. In a medium mixing bowl, whisk together the eggs, rendered animal fat, salt and pepper.

3. Add the baking powder and tapioca flour, whisk until smooth.

4. Add the cheese, whisk until well combined.

5. Grease a muffin pan with olive or grapeseed oil.

6. Pour mixture into muffin pan, filling cups to about ½ inch from the top.

7. Bake at 375 degrees for 20 min, turning the pan once during cooking. Muffins should release from the pan fairly easily.

Yield: 6 muffins.

Breakfast Egg Salad

Egg salad for breakfast? Why not? This handy quick meal has everything you love about paleo breakfast: eggs, meat, fat and tons of flavor. So as long as the idea of a cold egg dish doesn't weird you out, this one is sure to be a hit for those days when you're in a hurry. Just make a batch early in the week and you'll have it whenever you need it.

Ingredients:

6 large eggs, hard boiled
4 slices uncured bacon, chopped
¼ cup paleo mayo
1 tbsp finely minced onion
salt and pepper to taste

Directions:

1. Dice the eggs with an egg slicer or by hand.

2. Chop and fry the bacon until crispy.

3. Mix the eggs, bacon, onion and mayo. Season to taste with salt and pepper

4. The result is a creamy crunchy protein-bomb that will keep you going until lunch. Serve with sliced vegetables or almond crackers for dipping.

Yield: 2-3 servings.

Taco Fritatta

Fritatta is one of the easiest egg dishes there is. It's just a process of throwing a few ingredients into a pan, covering with beaten eggs and throwing it in the oven for a few minutes. The result is an easy to eat, easy to love dish that is as good cold as it is fresh out of the oven. You can make this ahead if you're usually hurried in the morning, or you can whip it up, go brush your teeth and comb your hair, and when you come back breakfast will be done!

Ingredients:

½ pound ground beef
2 tbsp taco spice mix (check out chapter 2 for the recipe)
½ onion, finely diced
½ red bell pepper, finely diced
1 small jalapeno, ribs and seeds removed, diced
1 clove garlic, minced
6 large eggs
1 tbsp coconut milk
Salt and pepper, to taste

Directions:

1. Pre-heat the oven to 350 degrees.

2. In a large, oven-proof skillet over high heat, brown the beef with the taco seasoning. When the beef is almost browned, add the onions, peppers, garlic and jalapeno. Cook until the beef is done and the veggies are slightly charred.

3. In a measuring cup, beat together the eggs, coconut milk, salt and pepper.

4. Turn the stove top off and stir the eggs in with the beef mixture. Transfer the skillet to the oven.

5. Cook for 10-15 minutes at 350 degrees, until the edges are starting to crisp up and the middle is completely cooked. Remove from oven and allow to cool 5-6 min, until the edges pull away from the pan. Invert onto a serving dish or cutting board and slice.

Yield: 4 servings.

Sausage and Kale Fritatta

Fritatta has a lot of possibilities, so we though we'd explore a few more. After you figure out what you like in them (and it can be *anything*, really), we're willing to bet you eat a couple of these a week. It's just the simplest way to get a good breakfast in your body before you leave the house. This recipe is a nutrient-packed start to any day.

Ingredients:

½ pound breakfast sausage
2 cups kale, chopped, large ribs removed
1 clove garlic, minced
6 large eggs
1 tbsp coconut milk
Salt and pepper, to taste

Directions:

1. Pre-heat the oven to 350 degrees.

2. In a large, oven-proof skillet over high heat, brown the sausage. Add garlic and kale and cook 2-3 min, until kale is slightly wilted

3. In a measuring cup, beat together the eggs, coconut milk, salt and pepper.

4. Turn the stove top off and stir the eggs in with the sausage and kale. Transfer the skillet to the oven.

5. Cook for 10-15 minutes at 350 degrees, until the edges are starting to crisp up and the middle is completely cooked. Remove from oven and allow to cool 5-6 min, until the edges pull away from the pan. Invert onto a serving dish or cutting board and slice.

Yield: 4 servings.

Chili Chicken Fritatta

Yep, one more fritatta recipe. Trust us, it's worth trying. Chicken is probably not your first thought at breakfast, but after you give this a whirl, you'll start rethinking your breakfast assumptions. And after you've tried all three of the fritatta recipes in this book, you'll have a glimpse of just how wide the world of fritatta is.

Ingredients:

1 boneless, skinless chicken breast (6-10 oz), fully cooked
1 tbsp chili powder
2 tbsp ghee
1/2 onion, diced
2 tomatoes, diced
6 large eggs
1 tbsp coconut milk
Salt and pepper, to taste

Directions:

1. Pre-heat the oven to 350 degrees.

2. In a large, oven-proof skillet over high heat,

melt the ghee. Add onion, sautee 3-5 min, until tender. Add tomatoes, cover and sautee 4-5 min, until tomatoes are beginning to break down.

3. Add chicken and chili powder. Stir until everything is evenly distributed.

4. In a measuring cup, beat together the eggs, coconut milk, salt and pepper.

5. Turn the stove top off and stir the eggs in with the chicken mixture. Transfer the skillet to the oven.

6. Cook for 10-15 minutes at 350 degrees, until the edges are starting to crisp up and the middle is completely cooked. Remove from oven and allow to cool 5-6 min, until the edges pull away from the pan. Invert onto a serving dish or cutting board and slice.

Yield: 4 servings.

PALEO

SNACKS

Okay, it's confession time. This chapter kinda got wedged in here.

Snacks are totally comfort foods, right? Of course they are. Truth is that the best paleo snacks don't really require recipes; fruit, veggies, hard boiled eggs, things you don't need us to tell you about. There are, however, a few snacky ideas worth jotting down, so we had to do a few. But... there's only three of them here.

Why bother dedicating a whole chapter to this? Why not just wedge them in somewhere else? Well, we just didn't think they fit anywhere else, but we also didn't think this book would really be complete without them. So here they are, your three paleo snack recipes!

Herbed Almond Crackers

Sometimes you just need a cracker. It's the best thing to dip in tuna salad, heavy party dips and the like. And you need your cracker to be something with enough flavor to stand on its own, yet subtle enough to allow whatever you dip it in to shine through.

This, friends, is that cracker.

Ingredients:

1 pound raw almonds
2 large eggs
2 tbsp grapeseed oil
1 tbsp sea salt
1 tbsp black pepper
2 tsp dill weed
1 tbsp fresh parsley, chopped
1 tbsp fresh tarragon, chopped

Directions:

1. Preheat the oven to 350 degrees.

2. In a food processor, grind the almonds until

they form a coarse powder.

3. Add all remaining ingredients and pulse to combine. Remove from food processor and form into a large dough ball.

4. Take half the dough and place it between two sheets of parchment.

5. Flatten with your hands, then roll thin with a rolling pin. Remove top layer of parchment, then carefully and quickly invert onto a well-greased sheet pan. Cut into squares using a knife or pizza cutter.

6. Bake at 350 degrees for 12 minutes. Remove from oven and allow to cool completely before removing from the pan. Serve with your favorite dip, condiment or as a side for lunch.

Yield: about 6 servings.

Beef Jerky

Even if you don't have a dehydrator, you can make great beef jerky at home! It takes a while, but the results are totally worth it. Ever had a jerky that was too tough, or maybe not tough enough? When you make your own, the toughness and flavor are up to you.

Ingredients:

2 pounds of very lean beef (top round is good, or well-trimmed flank steak)
¼ cup coconut aminos
1 tbsp black pepper
1 tsp salt
1 tsp garlic powder
1 tsp onion powder
1 tsp crushed red pepper (optional)

Directions:

1. Place thawed beef in the freezer for 30 min to help firm it up.

2. Slice beef into 1/4" thick strips. If you prefer jerky that is easier to chew, cut

217

against the grain, or diagonally. If you prefer your jerky very tough, cut along the grain. Make sure to trim away *all* fat. Fat will go rancid when making jerky.

3. Place beef in a glass baking dish and cover with the remaining ingredients. Stir to make sure everything is well coated. Refrigerate uncovered at least overnight, up to 24 hours.

4. Arrange strips of beef on a wire rack above a baking sheet with raised sides. Bake at your oven's lowest setting with the door partially opened. Check periodically, meat may take up to 4 hours to dry completely. Store in a zip-top bag for up to 2 months.

Yield: 10-12 oz.

Multi-Nut Butter

Peanuts (and therefore peanut butter) may not be paleo, but most other nuts are. In fact, most "nuts" are; the peanut is in fact a legume, and legumes are definitely out because our bodies have a very tough time digesting them.

You can buy almond butter, cashew butter, even sunflower seed butter, and all of these are great. But if you're looking for something a little different, a little more adventurous, try recreating the unique blend of flavors found in a can of premium mixed nuts. When whipped into a nut-butter, there's nothing like it!

Ingredients:

8 oz almonds
8 oz pecans
8 oz cashews
4 oz walnuts
4 oz Brazil nuts
3 tbsp sunflower seeds
1 tbsp salt

Directions:

1. Dry roast your nuts by arranging them on a sheet pan and baking for 10-15 min at 350 degrees.

2. Add nuts and salt to a food processor and process until nuts become buttery. This can take up to 10 min. Nuts will go through 3 distinct stages; ground nuts, flour and butter. Be patient and it will come together.

Yield: about 32 servings

PALEO

DESSERTS

A book about comfort food wouldn't be much good without dessert, would it? Luckily paleo desserts come in all shapes and sizes, and are sure to satisfy your cravings.

The main difference with paleo desserts is that instead of relying on processed sugars and heavy syrups, paleo desserts are designed to coax out the natural sweetness and goodness of fruits and other great ingredients.

Even so, this is where we encounter some of our most challenging paleo gray areas. If you don't tolerate natural, raw honey in your diet, then some of these might nor work for you. Even if you're the most tolerant paleo person out there, it is still advisable to enjoy these recipes in moderation.

So without further ado...

Grilled Bananas

This recipe is a perfect compliment to any grilled meal. Bananas are naturally sweet, especially if you use nice, ripe bananas. You don't want them quite banana-bread-ripe, but a solid yellow with a few brown specks will deliver a perfect treat.

Ingredients:

4 large bananas, halved lengthwise
2 tbsp ghee, melted
1/2 tsp ground cinnamon
1/4 tsp ground nutmeg
1/8 tsp ground ginger
1/8 tsp ground cloves
1/8 tsp ground allspice
2 tbsp raw, organic honey (if tolerated)

Directions:

1. Preheat the grill to medium heat.

2. In a small bowl, mix together the spices until uniform. Sprinkle over the bananas

3. In a measuring cup, whisk together melted ghee and honey (if using). Drizzle mixture over bananas.

4. Grill the cut side of the banana for 2-3 min, until it's nice and caramelized. Eat with a spoon right out of the peel.

Yield: 4 servings.

Almond Cookies

In this recipe we dip into another one of our Paleo gray-areas... dark chocolate! Strictly speaking, even very dark dark chocolate isn't Paleo; it does contain some sugar. But chocolate that is 85% cocoa or higher is awfully close.

Chocolate itself is just a mixture of cocoa butter and cocoa solids, both of which are naturally derived from the cocoa bean. Extra-dark chocolate eschews the use of milk in favor of things like bourbon and vanilla beans. So there may be a few questionable ingredients, but they're generally kept to a bare minimum. These cookies are one of those in-case-of-emergency recipes. They're tasty enough to keep you from going off the deep end.

Ingredients:

1 pound almond meal
2 eggs
2 tbsp ghee, melted
1/2 tsp cinnamon
1/4 tsp nutmeg
1/4 tsp allspice
pinch salt
12-14 oz dark chocolate (about 4 bars)

Directions:

1. Preheat the oven to 350 degree

2. In a food processor, pulse together the almond meal, eggs, ghee, cinnamon, nutmeg and allspice until a dough forms.

3. Place the dough between two sheets of parchment and roll flat with a rolling pin. Remove the top sheet of parchment. Quickly and carefully invert the cookies onto a well-greased sheet pan. Cut into squares using a pizza cutter or a knife.

4. Bake at 350 degrees for 12-14 minutes. Remove your cookies from the oven and allow to cool completely.

5. Make a double boiler by positioning a glass mixing bowl atop a saucepan filled with about 1" of boiling water. Add the chocolate and whisk until smooth. Extra dark chocolate will take longer to melt than milk chocolate.

6. Dip each of the cooled cookies halfway in the chocolate. Place on a fresh sheet of parchment and allow to cool at room

temperature until chocolate is firm. This
may take up to 2 hours.

Yield: about 40 cookies

Banana Coconut "Ice Cream"

Now, ice cream, technically, has to be cooked with eggs, otherwise it's sherbet at best. But this little recipe is close enough to fool the part of your stomach that calls out for it's favorite frozen treat.

Ingredients:

4 large ripe bananas
1 cup coconut milk
1/3 cup unsweetened shredded coconut
1/4 cup raw, organic honey (if tolerated)

Directions:

1. Add all ingredients to a food processor and blend until smooth.

2. Seal in an airtight container and freeze for 2 hours.

Yield: 4 servings.

Coconut Berry "Ice Cream"

Here's another flavor of icy treat that will satisfy your cravings and cool you down on a hot day.

Ingredients:

2 cups coconut milk
1/4 cup raspberries
1/4 cup blackberries
1/2 cup blueberries
1/4 cup raw, organic honey (if tolerated)

Directions:

1. Add all ingredients to a food processor and blend until smooth

2. Run mixture through a mesh strainer to remove any seeds.

3. Seal in an airtight container and freeze for 2 hours

Yield: 4 servings.

Apple-Berry Popsicles

There's something about a popsicle that takes you back to childhood. These popsicles might not turn your tongue funny colors (after all, it's the artificial dyes that do that!) but they're sure to keep the kids – and you – happy.

Ingredients:

1 large bottle of unsweetened, all natural apple juice
1/3 cup raspberries
1/3 cup blackberries
1/3 cup blueberries
1/2 cup strawberries, sliced

Directions:

1. Add berries to a blender or food processor and blend until smooth.

2. Spoon berries into a popsicle mold. Fill with apple juice and insert the sticks.

3. Freeze 2 hours, or until all popsicles are frozen.

Yield: 6-12 popsicles.

A Final Word of Encouragement

So there we have it. 101 great recipes that you will love to cook (and even more, love to eat!) for years to come.

The Paleo diet has so much to offer, and the amazing benefits you will experience as you go for it will increase your health, your vitality (and your waistline).

I am so glad that I have been able to share my favorites with you!

Made in the USA
Lexington, KY
18 January 2014